HYDROPONIC GARDENING
FOR BEGINNERS

Contents

Introduction

Hydroponics is a technique to grow plants and food without the presence of soil. In this technique, all the necessary elements for the growth of plants are provided at some other places like rooftops of houses or buildings. This practice has been followed for quite a long time. But it has not gained greater currency that it should have. People, in some countries, grow plants, vegetables, and fruits on their roofs with the help of hydroponics technique. This is the recent development in the field of horticulture. Hydroponics may be used to solve the problems of food shortage and scarcity of food supplies due to various factors which have led to the reduction of cultivable land.

Currently, the population has been increasing tremendously. This is leading to the usage of arable land for habitation purposes on large scales. Due to this reason, there has been a more significant reduction in the soil available for cultivation. This may ultimately lead to a shortage in the food supply. In these circumstances, the field of hydroponics assumes greater importance. As by growing vegetables and fruits themselves, everyone may become self-sufficient and increase the productivity of food, thereby relieving pressure on national and international supplies of food. Hydroponics, when compared to regular gardening on soil, has various advantages and may be helpful in the current circumstances. It may be resorted to as a hobby or extra-curricular activity by those people living in urban centers where it is very much difficult to find land for cultivation or gardening.

Though hydroponics has not been practiced commonly yet, it is one of the required fields of the near future. Therefore, it is very much necessary that people are made aware of this technique of growing plants in the absence of cultivable land. In this regard, this is an attempt to bring awareness among people regarding the various aspects of hydroponics and its significance in the evolving situation. It is effortless to grow plants at your rooftop without soil. Only a little knowledge is required to achieve this goal. In pursuit of that goal, this comes with every necessary detail necessary for beginners to grow fruits and vegetables for themselves at their homes.

This will impart the basic knowledge of becoming an expert in hydroponics. However, it depends on the interests of the readers how much keenness they show to learn this technique. This write-up may stimulate the attention of readers, and hydroponic gardening may become one of the most interesting extra-curricular activities for the readers, along with the provision of the necessary food supplies.

What is Hydroponics gardening

Two Greek words, "hydro" mean water and "ponies," mean work which are used to describe hydroponic. For thousands of years, there has been a definition of soil-less planting or hydroponics. Two examples of hydroponics have been the suspended Gardens of Babylon and The Floating Gardens of the Chinese. About 1950, scientists started to experiment with soil-less gardening. Since then, hydroponics has been used in crop production in other countries such as Holland, Germany, and Australia, with excellent results.

Many civilizations in history have employed hydroponic techniques. The hanging gardens of Babylon (the Aztecs of Mexico) and the floating gardens of the Chinese are examples of the culture "Hydroponic. Egyptian hieroglyphic records from several hundred years B.C. depict cultivation in the water. While hydraulics is an ancient plant growing system, As noted by the Howard M. Resh in Hydroponic Food Production.

Over the last century, scientists and horticulturalists have observed different hydroponics methods. In non-Arabic areas of the world and regions with little to no soil, one of the possible applications of hydroponics that has led to work is increasing fresh goods. Hydroponics was used to supply new products generated in local hydroponic systems to troops stationed on non-Arab islands in the Pacific.

Hydroponics was integrated into the space program subsequently throughout the century. When NASA took note of how life would be situated on another planet or in the duration of the World War 2, the Earth's moon, hydroponics comfortably incorporated into their development programs. By the 1970s, hydroponics has not only interested researchers and analysts. The benefits of hydroponic agriculture attracted Modern farmers and enthusiastic hobbyists.

There are many benefits of hydroponics, some of them are:

•It has the potential to produce higher yields than conventional agriculture based on soil.

• It has the power to enabling food production in areas of the world that do not sustain soil crops to be grown and eaten.

• Eradication of the need to make our air, water, soil, and food cleaner effectively (which means most pests live in the soil).

Commercial farmers flock like never before to hydroponics. The goals of these emerging strategies concern issues, such as helping people to end poverty in the world and clean up the environment. People around the world have designed or purchased their systems to allow their family and friends to enjoy fresh and nutritious food. Ambitious people are trying to fulfill their aspirations by selling their goods to local markets and restaurants, making their living in their greenhouses. In the classroom, educators understand the excellent application of science and gardening that hydroponics can offer children.

Chapter 1: Introducing Hydroponics

The Theory Behind Hydroponics

Many people think that the practice of hydroponics is entirely a modern-day invention, but this is not true. Hydroponics is a practice that has its roots deep in history. Researchers believe that it has existed for centuries, however, it was not recognized as a significant agricultural breakthrough as it is today. Just remember the famous and age-long Babylonian hanging gardens and the Aztecs (Mexico) floating gardens where plants were grown with water, oxygen, and other nutrients without necessarily planting such plants in soil.

Even records from the Egyptian hieroglyph states that plants were grown in water hundreds of years B.C. The "Hanging Gardens" are described as one of the "Seven Wonders of the Ancient World". This garden was nurtured through a dedicated water system that got its source from a river stream that was rich in nutrients and oxygen. In 604-562 BC Nebuchadnezzar II built the "Hanging Gardens" around the Eastern bank River Euphrates for Amyitis, his wife. With more refining through science, hydroponics can be practiced by almost everyone and everywhere today.

How the Hydroponic System Works

In contrast to traditional agriculture, where the soil provides support to the plant allowing it to remain upright and providing a supply of nutrients, in hydroponics plants have artificial support and a solution containing all the required nutrients is provided. The idea behind the hydroponic setup is simple. Environmental factors often limit plant growth, and therefore, by providing a solution that contains nutrients to the plant's roots, the gardener provides a constant optimal supply of nutrients and water. The nutritional efficiency makes a plant live up to its potential by making it more productive.

The nutrient-rich solution is delivered in several ways:

● Firstly, the plants are placed in an inert substance, as mentioned earlier, and its roots are occasionally flooded with the solution.

● Secondly, the plants could be placed on the inert substances and the solution rained on the plant using a solution dripper.

● The third option places the plants on a film that slightly slopes, and this allows the solution to trickle down to the roots of the plants

● The fourth way has the plant and its roots suspended in the air, and the roots are occasionally sprayed with the solution mist.

All the methods described above use machines to do one thing or another, either using a mister, or using a pump to deliver the solution from its storage area. The solution must also be aerated so that the roots get the oxygen they require once the solution comes on. Plants need energy to absorb the minerals in the solution, and this absorption process requires energy, which is made possible by respiration.

Is It Hard?

Surely, setting up and maintaining a hydroponic system can be quite a difficult task without clear and complete directions. This is because the plants need a variety of nutrients, and each species' optimal amount of nutrients varies. In addition, each plant's nutritional requirements will change as it goes through various stages of development. Local conditions such as the hardness of the water that is used also matters a lot.

Moreover, some nutrients are absorbed into the plant much faster than others: this can cause a buildup of some ions in the solution, hence a change of the solution's pH. Once the pH is affected, the absorption of other nutrients by the plant is hindered because the uptake of some nutrients is pH-dependent, and because the excess availability of some nutrients prevents the uptake of others. For example, when the ammonia content is very high, the calcium uptake decreases, and on the other hand, too much calcium reduces the absorption of magnesium.

Another critical aspect to be careful about is that some elements react with one another, and form compounds that are difficult to absorb. This means that the elements must be provided at different times.

With the above different variations, a hydroponic farmer must have a good grasp of the requirements of plants and the interaction of nutrients with each other, and with the plants themselves. They must carefully monitor the solutions they provide to the plants and check to see the changes in concentration that could come about. The alternative option is for the farmer to invest in an automated hydroponics system, which is quite expensive, to run the process on his or her behalf.

Farmers are also obliged to take great care of the solutions they are using to keep them from contamination by unwanted substances. Most choose to enclose the hydroponic project inside a greenhouse or a building to ensure that they alone have control of what is going on in the systems. This limitation also gives the farmers the liberty to optimize on the environmental influences of the plant, such as the light, carbon dioxide exposure and the temperatures, all to maximize the yields received.

This means that hydroponics is just not about growing crops without using soil; it also means that the farmer has absolute control of the plants and their growing process, at least.

Crops You Could Grow

If you are wondering what kind of crops you can grow using the hydroponic system, the simple answer is that you could grow any vegetable, fruit or houseplant you want. The system, however, is best suited for crops that can grow well in hydroponic conditions.

The general rule is that hydroponics is the best solution for plants that tend to have shallow roots. For example, you could grow some lettuce, radishes, herbs, or some spinach. The aggregate systems are best suited for crops that have a deep root system like beetroot, and those whose tops tend to be heavy like cucumbers, and squash. Other crops you could plant include tomatoes, strawberries, peppers, celery, and watercress.

Tomato varieties are particularly popular in this kind of farming because it is said that they bring forth larger fruits and that they grow indeterminately, which is to say that they will grow continually and repeatedly. You will always find fruit on their stems.

Farmers also tend to lean towards the disease-resistant crop varieties because the plants live longer and hence produce for a longer time.

Avoid growing plants that are not genetically suited to the hydroponic environment like wheat. Researchers found that for you to grow enough wheat to make a loaf of bread, you would need at least $23! That's too expensive.

The Growing Systems

Many innovative systems have been created to replace the traditional gravel bed that was taken up when people first started embracing hydroponics. When making a decision on which growing system you would wish to install, ensure that you take into account the economics of your agribusiness, space requirements of the plants, the type of crops that you would be growing, the support system and the growing time.

Once you have figured these details out, you can then decide on whether you wish to grow these plants in a greenhouse or growth room. Some farmers take both options and will use the growth room for germination purposes, after which the seedlings that come off the process are transferred to the greenhouse where they grow out as crops. The added advantage of this arrangement is that the heat emitted from the lights in the growth room redistributes into the greenhouse, heating and warming the air in there.

Some of the common growing material farmers use include:

Pipes and Troughs

Farmers use PVC pipes or open and closed plastic troughs to grow cucumbers, lettuce, and tomatoes. The troughs are either filled with just the nutrient solution, or they may be filled with vermiculite, perlite or peat moss. Some farmers mount these pipes or troughs on movable racks or rollers to enhance their spacing as they grow. In the case of PVC pipes, farmers prefer the 3-inch diameter kind that has 6-inch holes on the center to give enough room for the development of lettuce leaves. Most of these troughs and pipes are 10 feet or 12 feet. The farmer then uses carts to move the pipes from the growing area to the packing room.

Stones or Sand Culture

This is the medium that is used for most of the plants that need a deep bed, that of about 18 to 23 inches. The bed is prepared by placing the pea stones, the trap rock, or the sand on a plastic-lined bed or trough that is sloping to one point to allow the excess nutrient solution to drain off. The minimum slope should be 2%. Once the farmer places the seedlings onto this medium, he then must water with the nutrient solution several times during the day.

Beds

Hydroponic beds are plastic lined bed-like structures where the nutrient solution is pumped from one end and flows to the other end. If you want to plant lettuce plants on beds like these, consider using foam polystyrene flats to help the plants float in the solution.

Trays

With this method, the trays are flooded with the nutrient solution periodically. The trays are suitable for growing crops that were started in 1 to 2-inch diameter growth blocks. Most farmers buy these plastic molded trays or those that are made from waterproof plywood.

Bags

Another option is to use polythene film bags and filling them with a solution made with peat and vermiculite. The bags are then laid up in a trough, from one end to the other, and soaker hoses or drip tubes are inserted in them to deliver the nutrient solution. These bags can be reused several times before they are discarded.

Besides the plant support material mentioned above, other materials could be required in order to complete your hydroponic systems. Farmers will need controls, tanks, and pumps. The tanks should be made of inert material, such as plastic, concrete, or fiberglass because if the tanks were made of some reactive material, the reaction between the tank and the fertilizer solution would corrode the tank, pipes, and pumps.

The farmer can have manual switches and controls as simple as a time clock or have a computer automated process where everything is adjusted automatically. The computer also adjusts the chemical content of the nutrient solution, in accordance with the nutrients that the plants are absorbing.

Chapter 2: Hydroponics vs Soil Gardening

So, what makes hydroponics so different from traditional soil gardening methods? Now, you are going to find it out. Here are the advantages of each type of plant growing concept.

Areas Where Hydroponic Gardening is Better

•Hydroponics prevents the overuse of fertilizer. Hydroponic plants are grown in a very controlled environment, where waste products are limited and less nutrient material is needed. The great thing about this control is that it allows less fertilizer to be used. This is especially beneficial for the humans and animals in the area, who will have less of a chance of drinking fertilizer-contaminated water.

•Hydroponics make better use of space and location. You can grow an indoor hydroponic system anywhere that you have room, because it takes up so little space and everything that the plant needs can be provided by your system. Additionally, roots grown in the soil need room to spread out while plants grown hydroponically have root systems that do not need to spread out. This means that you can grow plants closer together and save space.

•Hydroponics uses less water. You would think that a hydroponic growing system would use more water than traditional methods, but that is not true. When plants are grown hydroponically, they are given only the amount of water that they need. When you water plants that are in soil, some of the water will to seep into the ground or leak out of the pot. It will also be evaporated. Therefore, the plants are receiving only a fraction of the water that you are providing. Hydroponic systems are much more efficient when it comes to water usage and you actually end up using 70 to 80 percent less water.

•Hydroponic systems reduce weeds, pests, and diseases. When you use more traditional gardening methods, the soil that you grow in can be filled with diseases, pests, and other plant parts. Hydroponic systems get rid of these problems almost entirely.

•Hydroponic systems grow plants twice as fast as traditional methods. Do you know what that means? You can have several harvests each year. Because hydroponic systems provide exactly what the plant needs without the plant having to hunt for it, the growing cycle is much more efficient.

•Hydroponics makes it easier for you to control the quantity and the chemical composition of growing nutrients. Every plant, like every person, is unique. Each type is will thrive in certain environments and struggle in others. Hydroponics is fun in this way. You can adjust the amount of nutrients in the solution and adjust it until you have the perfect growth solution.

Areas Where Soil Gardening is Better

•Soil gardening has a lower initial cost. While hydroponic systems vary in their initial cost, they can get quite expensive. Some of these costs will be offset by the lesser amount of water, fertilizer, and pesticides that you will need.
•Soil gardening does not use electricity. In several hydroponic gardening techniques, you must use a light source. Additionally, some systems use electricity to create bubbles in the nutrient system to aerate the roots.
•Soil gardening has a less risk of mold and bacteria growth. One disadvantage of hydroponics is that plants are grown in a very moist environment. This leaves the plants susceptible to growth of mold and sometimes dangerous bacteria if enough precautions are not taken. We'll see later how to avoid these problems in your hydroponic garden.
Now that you understand the major ways that hydroponics differs from more traditional growing methods using soil, it is time to move on.

Why choosing hydroponics

Now that you have learned about the hydroponic system, how it works, its advantages and disadvantages, why should you follow through and set up your own hydroponic system? When you come to think about it, people have grown plants the normal way in the ground since the beginning of time. Why should you go against the norm and start hydroponic farming?

Actually, the benefits of hydroponics over traditional farming are incredible and widely documented. Considering the inherent challenges you might face in traditional farming, it makes sense to shift to hydroponics for your gardening needs. Hydroponics allows you the benefit of growing plants in places where traditionally it would be impossible to grow plants. If NASA can grow plants in space, you can grow plants anywhere!

Let's take a look at a country, such as Israel, for example. Israel is predominantly an arid area. Naturally, it would be impossible to grow plants in this type of climate. However, Israelis produce a wide variety of fruits and vegetables with hydroponics. The same can be said of Arizona. Using the knowledge of hydroponics residents can produce not only the food they need but also expand their cultivation and export the surplus.

If you are living in a typical urban area, you are aware of the challenge of land use and access. Getting available land for agriculture in urban centers is a problem, and where it is available, the land comes at insane prices. Since there is little or no space available to plant a garden, hydroponics comes in handy.

If you live in a remote area, you can grow the plants you need during the whole year. You do not need to worry about seasonal plants and vegetables, or the challenges involved in importing produce. If you live in an area where you don't receive a fair amount of consistent warmth, such as in Russia or Alaska, your growth seasons are much shorter than in other places. Hydroponic greenhouses can help you get to produce throughout the year.

The environmental impact is another reason why you should consider hydroponic gardening. Compared to traditional soil-based gardening you save up to 90% on water using hydroponics. How is this possible? In hydroponic you can recycle and reuse not only water but the nutrient solutions too. This is very beneficial in places that have severe water shortage.

As regards the effect on the environment, hydroponic gardening is very friendly: plants only need around 20-25% of the fertilizers and nutrients that you need in normal soil gardening. You also need little or no pesticides at all. This means that hydroponic gardening doesn't put under pressure the environment as much as traditional gardening would, and at the same time you can enjoy significant savings. Since you don't need to import products anymore, the other benefit for the environment is a reduction of gas emissions through transportation. You also spend a shorter time harvesting plants grown through hydroponics because their root system is not so complicated. All the nutrients they need are readily available. Considering all these factors, investing in hydroponics is a brilliant idea.

Chapter 3: How to Choose A Hydroponic System

One important thing that you need to figure out is the right system for your hydroponic garden. This is the system that helps you creating the best conditions for your plants. It will help the roots to get the perfect amounts of oxygen, water and nutrients that your plants need. With the passive system, you will rely on gravity to help keep the plants happy. There are several different options that you can choose with each of these systems and there is no better one than another, there is only the best for you. Some people like the idea of gravity because they don't have to do as much work, but you will have to worry about moving the nutrients around. The active option works nicely because you can let it go for some time, such as when you leave to go on a trip, and the plants will still be taken care of. Let's look at a few of the most popular options that you can choose in order to get the very best out of your hydroponic system.

Wick System

The first set up is called the Wick System. This system is by far the easiest of the six and has the simplest of designs for someone starting out. The design is made up of a passive type system with no moving parts. Since the wick system uses this passive set up, it makes it not only cheaper to start, but it is also easy to maintain.

The positive sides of these types of systems are many, but there are a few drawbacks as well. Plants that require a lot of water, or thirsty plants, such as tomatoes do not do well in these types of systems. When you are using a wick system the ideal plants to grow are typically quick growing plants, such as herbs, microgreens and lettuces. This is important to keep in mind when choosing a system based on what you plan to use it for. The key factor of a wick system is that it uses more than one wick that will deliver the water to the roots of the plants, from the reservoir. The setup of a wick system typically is made up of four components; grow tray, wick, aeration (air stone + pump) and reservoir.

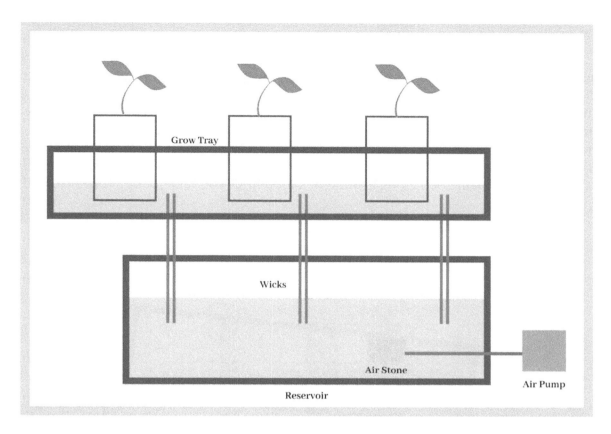

For you to really understand, it is important that we define the terminology that will show up from time to time. A wick, by definition, is a cord or thread of roughly woven, or twisted braids - something like a cotton rope, and this soaks up the liquid. So now that we know what the wick is, what exactly is the capillary action? This is the interaction between the liquid, in this case the nutrient-rich water, and the solid, the rope. The two meet and the liquid travels through the rope. This is how the liquid reaches the plant through the wick.

The growth tray with a wick system differs from all other setups because it uses a growing medium to entirely fill up a tray and does not use net pots. The growth trays can be anything that you use which is moveable and contain the mess of your plants, such as the substrate or medium. The kind of medium used should be one that drains slowly, allowing the full use of the capillary action. Each medium plays a key element in the support of your setup. Some of the most common mediums used are Perlite and Vermiculite. The reservoir with a wick system is basically the same as it is in any other hydroponic system. The reservoir is a large container containing fertilized water, which sits beneath the growth tray and feeds nutrient rich water to the plants.

The Nutrient Film Technique

So, the second system we will look at is the NFT. Inside of this system, you will find a tunnel. The plants will be placed on this tunnel while the roots are inside of it. You can then place your nutrient solution into the tunnel and while the nutrient solution travels through the system, it will make some contact with the roots of the plants.

When the nutrient solution gets through the system, it will not go to waste. Instead, there is a pump on this system that will recycle your nutrient solution, so it goes right back through your system again. It will keep going around in a loop until you take it out in order to add some new nutrients.

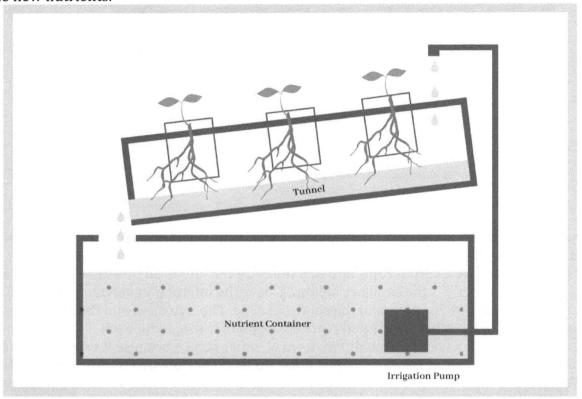

The biggest advantage that comes with this system is how it is completely enclosed. This helps to create a good level of humidity which the plants need to thrive. In addition, it reduces any risk for the roots to become dehydrated. This is also a good system to use for lettuce as well as microgreens and other short-term crops.

Water Culture System

With a water culture system, things are different. The water culture system works entirely on filling up a reservoir and using floating rafts to suspend plant roots into the nutrient-rich solution. It necessary to use simultaneously an air pump to flow oxygen to the plants. There is an ease of use with this type of system much like the wick system. There is only one piece of equipment to worry about, but you must pay close attention to your plants to avoid disaster. If there should be an issue with the air pump line, the plants can literally drown.

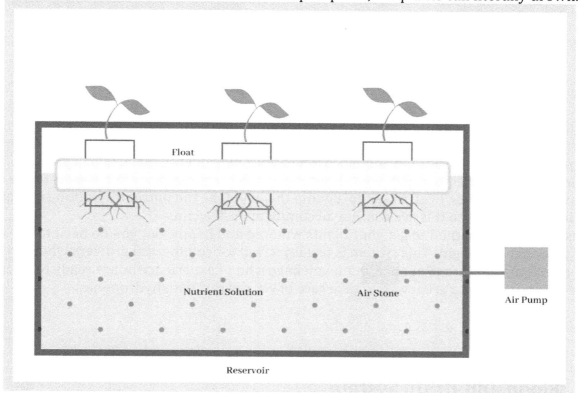

The key to making this system work is to make sure your air pump is always working. It may be beneficial to invest in a more expensive, better quality air pump if you can so that you can be sure that your pump will always be performing at its best. Unlike the wick system, the water culture system uses netted pots. A netted pot is usually a small black pot with holes that allow the free flow of water. As your plants grow, the nutrients in the water may need to be changed regularly as well.

Raft System

This is a good system for the beginner to choose because it is affordable and efficient. The plants will be put onto polystyrene sheets and then they'll float over the nutrient solution that you make. The roots of the plants will be exposed so they will get the nutrients and the water that they need. The solution inside of the area will be circulated so that oxygenation occurs. This is another good system to choose if you have a plant that goes through some rapid growth cycles.

Dutch Bucket System

Beginners can use this option, but commercial growers often save it to use it with specific crops. If you are planting a crop that takes longer to grow, such as roses, basil, peppers, and tomatoes, this is the system to choose because it does well with these kinds of plants.
This system will need a PVC pipe to use as your drain tube and a large bucket. You will take your premade nutrient solution and place it into your bucket with the help of a dropper. This solution is then drained out with your drainpipe into a prepared reservoir, thanks to the use of gravity. You will then need to set up a pump that will take the nutrient solution and push it back into the bucket, so this cycle is able to complete itself again.
This is an efficient method to get your plants watered and happy, but you do need to be careful and set it up right. This system is usually saved for commercial growers who have a lot of plants to take care of at once, but if you have a bit of experience or are ready to do the whole setup, it can be a great way to take care of your plants with hydroponics.

Flood and Drain System

The Ebb and Flow system is also known as the Flood and Drain system. Basically, what this means is that there is a growth tray holding your pots filled with a substrate of some kind. This could be clay pellets, wool or some other medium.
There is a timer on the system that will begin at regularly scheduled intervals, which will trigger the start of the pump and fill the reservoir. The reservoir will fill until it can reach the roots of the plants and then drains the water back down when it is finished. The regularly set timers keep the roots of the plants sporadically covered in nutrients and air.

Today Ebb and Flow systems are typically found in home gardens for the beginner, also much like the wick system. There are a few drawbacks that make the ebb and flow system less desirable than other systems. The most important is the fact that the roots tend to grow together, which means more work for the owner. They can spend more time than they would like to remove and harvest damaged plants. When you have this problem, the quality and yield of plants in these conditions are usually poor if not addressed. It can manifest in brown and yellow spots on the leaves as well.

Auto Pot Self-Watering System

Many of those who are interested in getting started with hydroponics are short on space and worry that they will not be able to complete this process. While it may take some time to get the Auto pot set up, you will find that it is a passive method to use and it is very good for plants that are slow at growing. This is a newer development so many people are not used to hearing about it, but the system does not take up a lot of space and is easy to use.
The nice thing about this process is that it can feed the plant on its own. This is possible thanks to the Smart Valve that can feed all your plants on demand; it will only release the water and nutrient solution when the plants need it, such as when the medium is going dry. This is also a great replication of natural rainfall, so you are getting the very best to your plants.

Drip System

The Drip System is the most widely used hydroponic system. It is set-up with a timer, a submerged pump and a grow tray. The timer is set to turn the pump on to allow the nutrient solution to drip off directly onto the plants through a tiny drip line. There are two kinds of Drip Systems: Recovery and Non-Recovery. In a Recovery Drip, the surplus nutrient solution that flows down is collected in a reservoir and re-used. In a Non-Recovery Drip, the nutrient solution that runs off is not collected.
The Recovery Drip System is more efficient and less expensive. Apart from being able to re-use the excess nutrient solution, the system does not need precise control for the watering cycles. The timer needs to be more precise in a Non-Recovery Drip System, so the plants get enough of the nutrient solution and there is minimal runoff.
The Recovery System requires more maintenance in recycling the solution back to the reservoir and the pH and strength of the nutrient solution needs to be preserved. This requires periodic testing and adjusting so that pH and strength levels do not shift. On the other hand, the Non-Recovery System needs less maintenance, as the solution is not re-used.

Aeroponics

Another system that you can use is the Aeroponic system. With this system, the plants get water and nutrients to the roots while they are in mid-air. To use this system, you will need to take the plants and place them into baskets that are on the top of an enclosure. The roots are exposed in this enclosure and then you can spray them with the nutrient solution. This is probably one of the most efficient methods to help take care of your plants. The roots are the only thing that you need to take care of, and they just need the solution that you are using. Anything that they don't use is will be recycled so it can be reused it later. You will need to be careful about keeping the right amount of humidity around the plants, so they stay hydrated as much as possible. Once you have this part done, you will find that the crops will grow so much faster compared to their counterparts that are grown using soil. In most cases, this process is best for those who are really limited on the amount of space they have, such as being in an apartment.

Picking the right system that works for your plants is going to take some research as well as reliance on your personal preferences. Sometimes it has to do with the amount of space that you have in your home. Check out these options to see how easy it is to make your own hydroponic garden without all the hassle while making it still work for your own personal use.

Chapter 4: What Can You Grow in Your Hydroponic Garden?

Now we know which are the basic setups for the hydroponic, how we can make several of them by our own and what kind of operation cycle we can expect to be going through. Here, we are going to look at the different plants that are available for us to grow. We will take a brief look at each plant to get an idea of how they best grow in our hydroponic setups. From there we will be looking at the ideal nutrition that our plants require.

Vegetables

When it comes to vegetables, there are a ton of options available to you. We'll be looking at a handful of these but first, let's tackle some general rules of thumb.
First up are those vegetables that grow underneath the soil. These are vegetables like onions, carrots and potatoes. These plants can still be grown in a hydroponic system but they require extra work compared to those that grow above the surface like lettuce, cabbage and beans. This means that those under-the-soil plants require a little more advanced skill, and you may want to get some experience with your hydroponic system before you try to tackle them.

The other rule of thumb is that you should try to avoid crops like corn and zucchini and anything that relies on growing lots of vines. These types of plants take up a ton of space and just aren't very practical crops for hydroponic systems. Instead of focusing on a plant type that isn't practical, you can make better use of our space and systems.

Beans

There are many different types of beans from green beans to pole beans, lima beans to pinto beans. Depending on the type of bean you plant, you may want to consider adding a trellis to your setup. Beans offer a wide variety for what you can add them to and they make a great side dish to just about any meal. When it comes to temperature, beans prefer a warm area. They also prefer a pH level of around 6.0.

If you are growing your beans from seeds, you can expect them to take between three and eight days to germinate. From there you can expect another six to eight weeks before it is time to harvest. After harvesting begins, the crop can be continued for about another three or four months.

Cucumbers

Like beans, there are a few different options when it comes to what kind of cucumber we can grow. There are thick-skinned American slicers, smooth-skinned Lebanese cucumbers, seedless European cucumbers. Such a wide variety, and the great news is they all grow pretty well in a hydroponic setup. Where beans prefer a warm temperature, cucumbers prefer straight-up hot. They like to be a step beyond just warm. They also prefer a pH level between 5.5 and 6.0

It only takes between three and ten days for cucumbers to begin to germinate. They take between eight to ten weeks to get ready for harvesting. When it comes to harvesting cucumbers, make sure that the cucumbers have taken on a dark green color and that they are firm when you grasp them. Because each cucumber grows at a different rate, you can expect the harvesting to take some time as you don't want to pick them before they are ready.

Kale

Kale is a delicious and nutritious vegetable that makes a great addition to just about any meal. There are so many health benefits to kale that it is often considered a superfood. Kale prefers a slightly cooler temperature; it grows best in a range between cool to warm. Like cucumbers, kale prefers a 5.5 to 6.0 pH level.

Seed to germination only takes four to seven days. However, to get harvesting takes between nine and eleven weeks. It is a little bit longer to grow kale than either beans or cucumbers but you can harvest it in such a way so that it continues to grow. If you only harvest 30% of your kale when it comes time, this lets it quickly regrow. Doing this means that you can easily keep this superfood in your garden and in your diet.

Lettuce

I would bet it is safe to say that no plant will pop up more often in our discussion than lettuce. This is because lettuce absolutely thrives in hydroponic growing conditions, which is great since lettuce can be used to make salads, give some texture and flavor to our sandwiches and burgers and is just an all-round versatile vegetable to have in the kitchen.

Growing lettuce offers a lot of variety. While lettuce prefers a cool temperature and a pH level between 6.0 and 7.0, it works in any of the hydroponic systems which you have made. For this reason, lettuce makes a great entry plant to get into hydroponics. Lettuce only takes a couple of days to germinate but the time to harvest depends on what kind of lettuce you decided on growing. For example, loose-leaf lettuce only takes forty-five to fifty days to get to harvest. Romaine lettuce can take up to eighty-five days.

Peppers

Like tomatoes, peppers are technically fruits, but they are so tightly linked to vegetable-based dishes and crops that many people think of them as vegetables. For that reason, we'll be looking at both peppers and tomatoes. Peppers share a lot of similarities to tomatoes in their growing preferences. Peppers like a pH level between 5.5 and 6.0 and a temperature in the range of warm to hot.

You can start peppers from seed or seedling. It takes about two to three months for your peppers to mature. When considering what kind of peppers to grow, know that jalapeno, habanero, mazurka, fellini, nairobi and cubico peppers all do fantastic in hydroponic growing.

Radishes

Radishes grow well in a setup with lettuce because both plants like cool temperatures and a pH level between 6.0 and 7.0.

What's very good about radishes is that they don't need any lights, unlike most plants. This means that if the cost of getting a light is too much for you right out the gate, radishes offer a way of trying out hydroponic gardening before dropping that cash. What's craziest of all is that radishes can grow super-fast, sometimes being ready to harvest within a month!

Spinach

Another plant that grows well in combination with lettuce and radishes is spinach. Spinach enjoys cool temperatures and a pH level between 6.0 and 7.0, so it fits in perfectly. It needs a little lighter than radishes do but it doesn't require very much at all.

It'll take about seven to ten days to go from seed to seedling with spinach and can be ready to harvest within six weeks. Harvesting can last up to twelve weeks depending on how you do. You can either harvest the spinach in full or you can pull off some leaves at a time. This makes spinach another great option for those first getting into hydroponic gardening.

Tomatoes

Okay, okay, we all know that tomato is technically a fruit. But we're looking at it here because together with the rest of the vegetables, add tomatoes and you have one great salad! Tomatoes will grow best in a hot environment and you will want to set up a trellis in your grow tray. They also like a pH level between 5.5 and 6.5.

Tomatoes come in a large variety; from the traditional ones we're looking at here through to those small cherry tomatoes that make delicious snacks. Germination can be expected between five to ten days and it will take a month or two before you begin to see fruit. You can expect it to take between fifty and a hundred days to be ready for harvesting and you will be able to tell by the size and color of the tomatoes.

Fruits

Nothing tastes sweeter than fruit that you have grown yourself. Hydroponic gardening offers a great way to grow some fruit inside the comfort of your own house. Like vegetables, there are many options available to us, but we'll be focusing on those that grow the best.

Blueberries

Great for snacks, baking and even adding vitamins to your morning meal, blueberries are a fantastic crop to grow. However, blueberries can be quite difficult to germinate from seeds, so it is recommended that you transplant blueberry plants instead. Blueberries are one of the slower plants to begin bearing fruit and can even take over a year to get to the point of producing. They like themselves a pH level between 4.5 and 6.0 in a warm climate.

Strawberries

The most popular of all the fruits that we can grow hydroponically, you can find strawberries being grown in smaller personal hydroponic setups and in the larger commercial growing operations. Preferring a warm temperature and a pH level of 6.0, strawberries grow best in a nutrient film technique system.

Strawberries that are grown from seeds can take up to three years to be ready for harvest, meaning that, like blueberries, they are a long-term crop. Together, blueberries and strawberries make for great fruit crops which can produce for several years if you are able to give them the growing time they need.

Herbs

Herbs make a great addition to any hydroponic setup. This is because it has been shown that herbs grown hydroponically have twenty to forty percent more aromatic oils than herbs that have been grown in a traditional soil garden. This means that you get more out of your hydroponic herbs with less used. This allows you to use less for the same end goal in your cooking, which means that your herbs will last you longer.

The best system for growing herbs is the ebb and flow system. Hydroponic herb gardens have been becoming a norm across the world because of their effectiveness. There are now even restaurants that grow their own hydroponic herb gardens on site because it is the most effective way to get fresh herbs of amazing quality.

Basil is the most popular of the herbs, with basil making up about 50% of the herb market in Europe. Both basil and mint like a warm environment and a pH level between 5.5 and 6.5. Similarly, chives prefer a warm to hot temperature and a pH sitting squarely around 6.0. This means that if you are careful with the temperature and pH level you can grow all three of these wonderful herbs in the same hydroponic setup.

An herb garden is a great way to get started with hydroponics. They can stay harvestable for incredibly long periods of time; they taste better than herbs grown in soil and make great additions to just about any meal. Not only that but herb gardens tend to be smaller than vegetable or fruit gardens and so a hydroponic herb garden will take up less space and can save some money in setup costs.

Chapter 5: Growing Plants in Hydroponic System

Types of vegetables

Cabbage

Cabbage is a cool-weather vegetable that thrives well on the environment. Cool-weather vegetables need special growing conditions. This means that the plants may have to be grown based on their natural seasons. To do this, adjust the temperature setting in the greenhouse based on the crops you want to cultivate.

Carrots

The easiest root crop to grow with the hydroponic system is carrot. Provide enough depth to allow them to expand. They are often cultivated in 5-gallon buckets but do well in other systems too

Potatoes

Potatoes produce small-sized tubers when they are grown with hydroponics. The potatoes most often do not match the sizes of its counterpart grown in the soil. Improvements are being carried out to meet up with the quality of the traditionally grown ones.
Apart from potatoes, other root crops do well if they are provided with enough depth. Do not forget that potatoes do most of their growth in their roots, foliage, and stem. Cramping them up to search for space will make them have stunted growth.

Onions

Onions can be grown in an outdoor system without hassles. Also, they can be grown in an indoor setting today. Onion seeds grow at a temperature of 65 - 70 for 6 - 10days. To make the growing system more complex for onions, use polystyrene, some very deep flowerpots, and soilless growing medium. Onions can even be grown on a windowsill.

Cucumbers

Hydroculture of cucumbers with your own hands will be very welcome in the economy if you want to get a good harvest of this vegetable quickly. Cucumbers are climbers, so it is better in small hydroponics to sow them along the wall of the pallet, and after the shoots appear, bind them to the installed at an angle stops. This method helps breeders looking for a way to grow cucumbers quickly. Such placement of cucumbers does not disturb other plants that may also be in this range, and the bound cucumbers eventually produce fruits of much higher quality. The optimal growth of cucumbers contributes to the bright day up to 14 hours.

Types of fruits

Tomatoes

Tomatoes do well in a hydroponic system. They need to be provided with a support system in the greenhouse hydroponic system just the same way it would be in a garden setting or a traditional greenhouse setting. There are varieties that grow bigger than the others so when selecting the type to grow, choose the one you can support better.

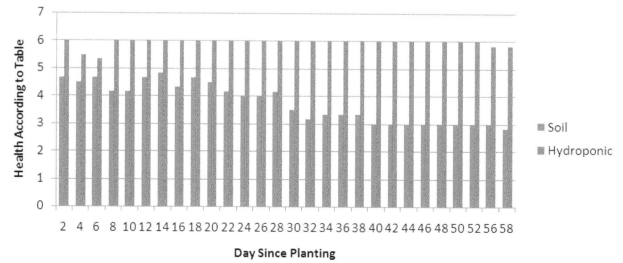

Effect of Use on Hydroponic Fertilizer Compared to Soil Grown on Health of Tomato Plants

Fruits and berries

Oftentimes small fruits and berries produce higher yield when they are grown in a hydroponic system. The large fruit trees can be nurtured in the hydroponic system before they are transplanted into soil. You shouldn't keep fruit trees in a hydroponic system when they are past the sapling stage.

Strawberries

Strawberries are among the berries commonly grown with the hydroponic system. It will take about 2-3 years for strawberries grown from the seed to mature, and it is not okay for hydroponic growers. But, the best kind to use is the cold stored certified virus tested runners. Strawberry runners are the sprouts of a mature strawberry plant that has been clipped and re-rooted. Do not use June bearers because they are appropriate for one heavy crop only. The best strawberries for hydroponic growers are the day-neutral or everbearing species.

Raspberries

Growing raspberries in a hydroponic system can be a little tricky, but they eventually yield well. Some species of raspberry are too large to even fit in a hydroponic setup, but the smaller varieties are good enough. What the smaller varieties lack in size, they make up for it in the high yield of raspberries that can be gotten.

Blueberries

Growing blueberries in a hydroponic system is not a bad choice if it can be done cost-effectively. This is because blueberries need acidic conditions when they are grown in soil but they have totally different requirements when grown in a hydroponic setup for them to produce well.

Types of plants

Lettuce

The downside of growing lettuce in a hydroponic system is that it matures very quickly. Sometimes, you may find that you have more lettuce than you could use. With as little as simple fluorescent lighting, hydroponics is bound to grow.

Kale

Any hydroponic setup is a good one for kale because it doesn't require special care. Plant starts to produce the seeds or cuttings that are used to plant kale. Other products that can be used for starting kale seeds include oasis cubes.

Spinach

Spinach favors cold weather and can only thrive in a hydroponic system when it is properly taken care of. It performs badly in high temperatures. The optimum lighting required for spinach is 12 hours. Other types of lighting like fluorescent lighting, high-pressure sodium, HID and others will work on spinach but the light should not be excessive.

Chinese Cabbage aka Bok Choy

This plant is a Brassica and can do successfully in hydroponics. It matures quickly and can be harvested just 30 days after germination. Proper cultivation can yield 3 harvests from one set of bok choy roots.

Types of herbs

Mint

A lot of mint varieties perform well in hydroponic greenhouse because they love wet conditions. Mints should be provided with enough space because of their spreading. Apart from this important requirement, your ginger mint, peppermint, spearmint or other types of mint should yield well for you.

Basil

Basil is a bushy annual plant that can grow up to 1 to 2 feet tall. Basil is another herb you can grow using a hydroponic system. Basil can be propagated either from the cuttings or from the seed.
The system provides adequate moisture for Basil to enhance its flavor. The yield of the Basil crop will definitely increase through hydroponic gardening. Other herbs are good too but make sure to check the growing conditions of any other plant before you plant.

Coriander

Coriander is a good herb to grow with hydroponics. It matures in around 4 weeks and can yield 2-3 harvests. You don't have to carry out any special procedure and extra lighting can make you have a bountiful harvest.

Chapter 6: The Growing Process

Here we will be covering the ins and outs of the growing process to make sure you are well briefed for every step of the way. When you combine this knowledge with your own system you'll be quickly on your way to creating an impressive assortment of crops in your hydroponic garden!

But before that, it is important to highlight that the conditions required will depend on what type of plant you decide to grow. This is a good time to have a recap on the general requirements:

•Reserve the temperature around the level that your plants require.
•Keep a moderate level of humidity.
•Use an effective source of lighting.
•Provide plenty of fresh air to your plants for adequate levels of CO_2.
•Provide oxygen to the root systems via a pump or agitation.
•Keep a consistent pH level.
•Keep a consistent concentration of nutrient solution.

For best results, I recommend doing specific research on the conditions require for your plant of choice, but here are some guidelines of favorable conditions for some popular choices:

Basil: High lighting, MH lamp, warm temperature.
Lettuce: Medium lighting, MH lamp, cool temperature.
Oregano: High lighting, MH lamp, warm temperature.
Parsley: High lighting, MH lamp, warm temperature.
Rosemary: High Lighting, 400/1000Watt lamp, warm temperature.
Strawberry: High lighting, 400/100Watt HPS lamp, warm temperature.
Tomato: High lighting, 400/100Watt HPS lamp, hot temperature.

Starting with Seeds

Seeds need to be started in a smaller separate area to your hydroponic system - when large enough, the plants will be transported to your main system.

The starting area should be a high humidity area with an appropriate starting medium. You can use propagation tray along with seed-warming mat to speed up germination.

To keep a high level of humidity you can use a dome over propagation tray.

As a starting medium, starter sponges, coconut fiber, or Perlite produce good results. The medium is then watered with a nutrient solution that is half the usual strength/concentration, and then kept moderately moist with the solution throughout the initial germination stage.

Below is a simple step-by-step process for successful seed starting:

1.Add moisture to your starting medium with half concentrated nutrient solution.
2.Insert seeds into the medium.
3.Ensure the temperature of the medium is between 72-80 degrees Fahrenheit.
4.Ensure the surrounding air is of a similar temperature.
5.Expose the area to soft light at first - increase this when the seeds have sprouted.
6.Keep the medium moderately moist with half strength solution throughout the starter stage.

Cloning from an Existing Plant

Another option you have is to start your growing process by making a clone from an existing plant. A growing tip is taken from another plant and replanted so that it can form its own roots in the growing medium. This will then grow into a plant that is identical to the plant it was taken from.

If you opt for the cloning process, the same conditions are required for seeds but only a 25 percent concentration of nutrient solution is needed. Here is a simple process to get you started:

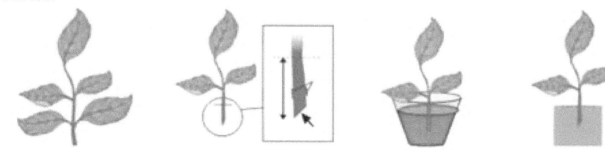

1.Select a healthy and green stem cutting from the plant of your choice - this should be approximately 3 to 5 inches.
2.Cut the tip off the plant using a clean and sharp knife.
3.Dip the tip into diluted nutrient solution.
4.Make another 45-degree cut from the initial cut.
5.Dip into a cloning root gel and then immediately into your starter sponge or medium.

The cutting now needs to be exposed to similar conditions to those of starting with seeds. The roots of the cuttings will develop within 1 to 3 weeks, after which they can be transferred into your main hydroponic medium.

Transplanting into the Main System

Once your seeds or cuttings have formed a noticeable root system, it is time to move them over to your hydroponic system. This is easiest with starter sponges - simply remove and insert the plugs into your main growing medium and you will be good to go. But if you're using looser starting mediums I recommend using basket liners to make the process much smoother.

Once they have been carefully transplanted with their roots embedded into the medium, provide them with a lower than normal light exposure. This light intensity can then be increased after 3 to 4 days.

Now by putting into practice everything you have learned about creating a perfect growing environment, you will be on your way to having your own charming selection of crops.

Your Perfect Lighting Solution

Lighting plays a crucial role for plant growth, and therefore will be an important part of your hydroponic growth system. Through a process called photosynthesis, plants convert light - which is from the sun in nature - into sugars that energize a plant's growth. This is a result of chlorophyll located in the leaf cells that uses light and combines this with carbon dioxide and water - the result is sugar and oxygen that is metabolized and transformed into energy for growth.

This makes the quality of the light you use vital for the prosperity of your plants. What we must aim to do within our hydroponic setup is to emulate the light that the sun produces with an artificial light source. Let's explore how you can best achieve this to guarantee positive results.

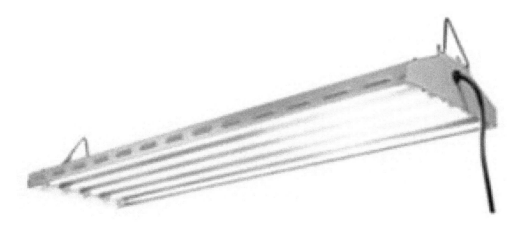

I strongly recommend using High Intensity Discharge (HID) Lighting for your growing efforts. It is widely agreed that this is a viable alternative to natural sunlight and is certainly much more effective than the generic grow lights that you often come across. By providing the correct quality and amount of light, HID lighting has been specifically designed to produce the strongest photosynthesis reaction. And fortunately, it is becoming increasingly accessible and affordable for the everyday hydroponic grower.

Intensity, Duration, and Color

For an optimal photosynthesis reaction, plants require 20-50 watts per square foot, depending on how much your chosen plants rely on light. Your HID lamp will have a wattage rating and this will determine the distance your lamp should have from your plants. Here is a general guide: 250Watt lamps should be approximately 12 inches from your plants, 400Watt lamps should be approximately 20 inches from your plants, and 1000Watt lamps should be at least 24 inches from your plants.

For maximum results, it is recommended to use paint in your growing area that has an eggshell finish - this increases the amount of light available for your plants. You can use a portable light meter to ensure your growing area is evenly lit throughout. Your plants will need different durations of light, depending on what you are growing - this is generally between 16 and 18 hours of light in a 24-hour time period.

Chapter 7: A Guide to Hydroponic Growing

Environments

Hydroponic cultivating has many advantages over traditional methods and is useful for the earth. Hydroponic growing uses less soil. Topsoil erosion doesn't become possibly the most important factor since hydroponic planting systems utilize no topsoil. The use of water is a fraction of what is needed in conventional gardening because the water is reused along with the nutrient solutions. This reusing and recirculation of the water and nutrients mean less water and healthier plants.

Fewer pesticides are necessary for hydroponic crops - or they're not required at all since your gardens can be grown indoors in controlled environments. This is great for people living in parts of the country with extreme weather conditions. Because hydroponics can be used indoors you can adjust the temperature as you normally would for yourselves. It would be impractical at best, to maintain optimal growing conditions outdoors but it becomes easy when using hydroponics. Progress has been rapid, and results obtained in various countries have proved it to be practical and to have several advantages over conventional growing methods.

Building on a good thing

Taking the science to the further action and growing on the success of your basic system include the use of manufactured sunlight in a closed environment- growing your plants in enclosed tents under hydroponic lights. With artificial lighting, your plants grow faster and bigger. With the tent, you can move your self-encased system to a different area with the least exertion. With the utilization of lights, the development cycle can be unsurprising and lengthened. The nutrients you feed your plant can be balance and altered for different purposes. For example, if you want to enhance your system with CO_2, your plants will grow even faster.

Finally, I have firsthand knowledge of a closed-loop commercial hydroponic system in practice and thriving in Milwaukee, WI. This group grows its produce and lettuce in warehouses under controlled lighting with the aid of manure from farm-raised fish in the system which fertilizes the greens. They grow this bounty and sell to local restaurants eliminating the need for trucking in produce and saving fuel, energy, and pesticides while their client eats fresh, local pesticide-free local fare with a fraction of the energy normally used.

Hydroponics, What A Way to Grow

An ever-increasing number of individuals nowadays are understanding that the above explanation is valid. Hydroponics is the best, cleaner and increasingly controlled approach to grow. From your prize flowers' blooms to the sparkling fresh taste of the salad you just picked to the satisfying taste of your fresh vegetables picked and eaten the same day. I say you can do it better with hydroponics.

In the method of soil gardening, the plant's roots dig and search into the soil for their needed nutrients whereas in hydroponic growing the exact nutrients designed to each plant's requirements are supplied and controlled in an automatically timed feeding.

It follows that as the plant doesn't have to work as hard for their nutrients the results are more energy being supplied to produce lush blooms for flowers and healthier more abundant vegetable crops.

Why not soil gardening

So often these days soil has become depleted from overuse and contaminated with harmful chemicals. In other words, it is not dependable for healthy produce. With hydroponic growing, there are no worries about lack of nutrition in your hydroponic grown vegetables and fruit and no worries about you or your family consuming pesticide or other chemical residues while you are eating the food. The main thing that gets into your hydroponic grown food is the thing that you put into it.

How to start your hydroponic garden

A small easy to use the complete hydroponic system for home use is easy to get on-line and quite affordable, too. Easy and fun to set up, the systems come complete with all that you need to get started together with all the how-to instructions and guidelines for success. There are even videos on YouTube that educate one on nutrient supply and explain the set-up of the systems. Quality producers here in the United States are remaining by prepared to help in any capacity they can with specialized help or parts substitutions if necessary.

An indoor hydroponic garden can easily become a child's or family project. How about a science project?

What kind should you get?

That depends solely on how much and what you want to grow. There is a wide delightful variety of hydroponic indoor garden systems to choose from. The systems come in different sizes from the small 6 planters such as "Emily's Garden System" all the way to the "Aeroflo2 - 60" which is expandable from 60 to 120 plant sites. Some of the "Aeroflot" series are long and narrow and fit easily along with a window for the natural sunlight. Then there is the "Ebb Monster" which is used for growing berries or fruit trees or larger vegetable varieties. There are some systems that double for plant cloning and/or plant cultivation.
So, you see, whatever you want to grow whether it be carrots, tomatoes, kale, flowers, citrus, berries, peppers, the hydroponics people have you covered.
Whatever your desires or goals there are systems to go along with it.

Now you have it! Where will you place it?

Some people think closet growing works best for them. It is relatively easy to control lighting and temperature in a small closet area. No drafts, etc.
Some, like me, prefer their garden out in the open to watch and enjoy maybe as a focal point as you would place or use a pretty house plant. On the top of an end table or corner table or dining room table. Some people have a complete vegetable garden set up inside their garage. There are small indoor greenhouses available and affordable that work well in a garage environment: controlling temperature, humidity, and light.

What about light?

Outdoor growing, of course, depends entirely on the sunlight. Indoors it works well also if you have placed your hydroponic system near a window or in a well-lit inside the porch. If not, you could consider something like the affordable and efficient Jump Start Lighting System which comes in two convenient sizes, 2 feet and 4 feet in length, and is entirely portable with a T5 fluorescent light bulb that can simulate the sun.

Nutrients! How to know which one to use?

Easy! Nutrients are usually included with each new system along with amounts of guidance. The manufacturers of the nutrients offer much instructional guidance and how-to. Again, there are videos to explain the use and amount. There are wonderful liquid plant nutrients available all the way from encouraging your flowers to have larger more frequent and colorful blooms to help your fruits and vegetables blossom earlier and more abundantly. There are nutrients to make your berries, grapes, and citrus taste sweeter.

Where will you get your plants to place in your new indoor hydroponic garden?

You can always grow them from seeds as usual. There is help out there for that also. A Germination Station or Hot House Plus is a great help in the sprouting of seeds. Most of the seedling/germination kits have heat mats and humidity domes to make sure of your success by making the ideal environment for your seedlings to increase their growth rate.

Or if you want to skip the seedling part of the deal you can get a new plant directly from rooting cuttings of your neighbor's or friend's thriving plants.

Chapter 8: Getting Started with Your Hydroponic Garden

Essential Parts of The Hydroponic System

1.The Growing Tray (Or Chamber)

The growing chamber or tray is the place where the roots of plants will grow. This area provides the plant with not only the required support but also access to the nutrient solution via its roots. The growing tray also protects the plant from pests, heat, and light. The root zone should be kept cool (like naturally inside soil) and free from any source of light, as prolonged exposure of the roots to light can increase heat stress. The production quantity and quality of flowers and fruits will also be affected due to heat stress.

The size of the tray or the chamber will depend on the size of the system you're trying to build. It will also depend on the type of plant you're using as well. If you use bigger plants, then they need more space for the bigger roots for holding the plant to the growing tray. You can use any structure as a growing chamber, except it shouldn't be made from metal, otherwise, it can corrode easily and react with the nutrients. Perform your research if you want to get ideas about building the growing chamber or tray, for the hydroponic system.

2.The Reservoir

The reservoir is generally made of plastic which will hold the nutrient solution. The reservoir shouldn't leak and should be able to hold enough water for the plant to intake continuously. There should be no light entering the reservoir. If you need to make a reservoir lightproof, only painting it will not do. You can use bubble wrap insulation around the reservoir to avoid the entrance of light. This is to ensure that microorganisms and algae growth does not take place.

3.The Delivery System

The best way to create an effective delivery system is to use a combination of various connectors and tubes made from PVC (Polyvinyl Chloride), black or blue vinyl tubing and also standard connectors and tubing used for garden cultivation. The process of building will depend on the type of system you want to set up, but make sure that you use sprayers or drip emitters. These sprayers are perfect to deliver the nutrient solution evenly over the plants. This equipment can get clogged over time, so make sure you keep some alternatives to swap out the clogged ones.

4.The Growing Light

You can use either natural sunlight or artificial growing lights for your hydroponic system. Natural sunlight will always be recommended because it is free. But if your surroundings do not allow for much sunlight to pass through (or if it is a seasonal variation), then you may want to use artificial lighting.
These lights are much different than standard residential lighting equipment. They are designed in such a way that they emit various color spectrums, much like the sunlight. These varying wavelengths of light are used by the plants for the process of photosynthesis. Photosynthesis is the method by which plants make their own food and therefore, it leads to the production of flowers and fruits. Therefore, the growing light plays a huge role in the success of your hydroponic system.

5.The Timer

You can use standard everyday timers, which might do the job for you quite fine. But it is recommended to use 15 AMP timer instead of the standard 10 AMP. More the AMP number, the more heavy-duty rating it will have. You can also use one if you've set up your hydroponic system in exterior conditions, as these timers are water-resistant and come with covers.
Simple analog-type times will work great and you don't have to spend much on the digital versions. The reason is that if digital timers lose their power or get un-plugged, all your settings will be erased. Also, unlike the analog timers, the digital ones don't have ON/OFF switches.

6.The Pump

Air pumps are optional in most hydroponic processes. These pumps generally cost less and are beneficial for your system. These pumps can be obtained from aquarium shops. They help in pumping air (mainly oxygen) to the roots of the plants. The air from the air pump moves through the air stones and creates air bubbles that rise up the nutrient solution.

Essential tools for the hydroponic system

pH meter

pH is a measure of how acidic or how alkaline water is. A pH of 7 is neutral. pH levels that range from 1 to 6 are acidic, and levels from 8 to 14 are considered alkaline or basic. Different plants have their preferences regarding pH levels. To ensure the best possible growth, you need to have a way of testing and then adjusting the pH level of your water. A pH meter can be obtained from local hydroponics stores or online. You need to calibrate the sensor with the calibration powder that comes with the meter. A basic pH meter will cost you $10 to $20.

Don't use paper test strips for the water because they are inaccurate. Most of the time, a pH meter is offered in combination with a TDS or EC meter.

EC meter

Electrical conductivity is a measurement of how easily electricity passes through the water, the higher the ion content, the better it is at conducting electricity.

All water has ions in it. When you add nutrients to the water, you are increasing the ion content, effectively increasing the electrical conductivity.

EC or Electrical Conductivity is an integral part of the hydroponics equation. The simplest way of explaining this is as a guide to salts dissolved in water. Its unit is siemens per meter, but in hydroponics, we use millisiemens per meter.

In short, the higher the number of salts in the water, the higher the conductivity. Water that has no salt (distilled water) will have zero conductivity.

However, electrical conductivity needs are also affected by the weather. When it is hot, the plants evaporate more water. That is why you need to decrease the EC in hot summer months. In colder winter months, you need to increase the EC.

In warm weather, you need to decrease the EC.

In cold weather, you need to increase the EC.

An EC meter doesn't tell you the specific amount of which mineral or fertilizer is in the water. If you only use a nutrient solution using the right ratios, you shouldn't worry.

Just because it doesn't monitor individual nutrients, doesn't mean it is not useful. Salt levels that are too high will damage your plants.

You generally need to keep them between 0.8 and 1.2 for leafy greens and between 2 and 3.5 for fruiting crops like tomatoes. The source of the water can influence the EC reading.

Sometimes, you see the recommended nutrient levels listed as CF. CF is the conductivity factor. This is like EC, used in Europe. If you multiply EC by ten, you will become CF.

TDS meter

TDS stands for total dissolved salts. You may hear some hydroponics growers referring to the TDS and not EC. These are both used to determine the strength of your hydroponic solution. If you buy a TDS meter, there will also be an option to switch to EC readings.

It is crucial to understand that TDS is a calculated figure. TDS readings are converted from an EC reading. The problem occurs when you don't know which calculation method was used to produce the TDS; there are several different ones.

In general, EC and CF readings are used in Europe, while TDS is an American measurement. But, regardless of which measurement you choose to use, they are both effectively the same thing: a measure of the nutrient levels in your solution.

The NaCl Conversion factor

This is effectively measuring salt in the water. The conversion factor for this mineral is your micro siemens figure multiplied by any number between 0.47 and 0.5. You'll find most TDS meters use 0.5. This is the easiest one for you to remember and calculate. Most of the meters sold will use the NaCl conversion factor.

As an example, if you have a reading of 1 EC (1 milli Siemens or 1000 micro Siemens), you will have a TDS reading of 500ppm.

`1000 micro Siemens x 0.5 = 500ppm`

Natural Water Conversion factor

This conversion factor is referred to as the 4-4-2; this quantifies its contents. Forty percent sodium sulfate, forty percent sodium bicarbonate, and twenty percent sodium chloride. Again, the conversion factor is a range, this time between 0.65 and 0.85. Most TDS meters will use 0.7.

`1000 micro Siemens x 0.7 = 700ppm`

Potassium Chloride, KCI Conversion factor

This conversion factor is not a range this time. It is simply a figure of 0.55. Your EC meter reading 1EC or 1000 micro Siemens will equate to 550 ppm.

`1000 micro Siemens x 0.55 = 550ppm`

These are not all the possible conversion options, but they are the most common. The first, NaCl is the most used today.

Dissolved oxygen sensor

Plant roots need oxygen to remain healthy and ensure the plant grows properly. The dissolved oxygen sensor will help you to understand how much oxygen is available in the water and ensure it is enough to keep your plants healthy.

If plants don't get enough oxygen to their roots, they can die. A minimum of 5 ppm is recommended.

A dissolved oxygen meter will be expensive for the hobbyist to buy, especially when you are starting. That is why dissolved oxygen meters are generally not purchased by people who do hydroponics for fun. A good meter can cost you $170 to $500 for a reputable brand.

You do not need to invest in one if you oxygenate the water. Oxygenation of the water can be done by using an air pump with an airstone in the water tank. Depending on the method of growing, you don't need to aerate the water.

The dissolved oxygen in the water will be at its lowest during the summer. The water heats up, and the dissolved oxygen becomes less available. While your plants can do very well in winter, they might lack oxygen during summer.

Net Pots

In some systems, you will need net pots to hold the plants. This is mostly true for deep water culture (DWC), Kratky, wick systems, Aeroponics, fogponics, dutch buckets, and possibly vertical towers.

Make sure you get the net pots with a lip on top to keep them from falling through. The standard size for lettuce is two inches (five centimeters). If you want to use tomatoes with dutch buckets, six inches (fifteen centimeters) is recommended.

3 and 2-inch (7 and 5 cm) net pots

If you are creating a new system on a budget, there are a variety of other options that can be used instead of buying net pots. For example, plastic cups with lots of holes in them, or simply fine netting on a wireframe. Use your imagination!

6-inch (15 cm) net pots for a 5-gallon (18 liters) bucket

Germination tray and dome

You need to start seeds in a dedicated germination tray. Most of these trays are 10x10 or 10x20 inches (25x25 or 25x50 centimeters) and generally include a humidity dome. These trays are used to let your seeds germinate and keep the humidity high.
After the first true leaves appear, it is time to transplant them into your system.
Usually, this is after ten to fifteen days. The humidity should be between sixty and seventy percent, while temperatures should be 68-77°F or 20-25°C. A 10x10 germination tray with humidity dome.

Chapter 9: Starting with Seeds

It is most satisfying when you plant a seed and nurture it until it becomes a full-grown plant and provides you with the expected harvest.

Of course, it takes more effort to grow a plant from seed than it does from a seedling, you need to decide if this is your preferred method and discover the best way of starting seeds. Hydroponics is an excellent system for starting seeds as you have complete control over the elements your seeds are exposed to.

Seeds vs. Seedlings

For your first attempt at hydroponics, it is quicker to plant seedlings. However, controlling all the elements of the growing process includes controlling the seeds. If you decide to plant seeds, you will have complete control over the type and quality of the seed you plant. Put simply, you can have any variety of seed but not necessarily any variety of seedling. Seeds are generally easier to get hold of then seedlings.

The other consideration is the growing media. In hydroponics, you avoid using soil. However, unless you have a hydroponic center near you, the seedlings you purchase are likely to be grown in soil. This means carefully removing the soil to avoid contamination of your system. Unfortunately, washing them can damage the roots of the seedling.

Besides, seeds are cheaper than seedlings, allowing you more opportunities for failure without breaking the bank.

With proper planning and equipment, you are better off growing the plants from seed.

Starting Your Seeds

The best way to start seeds is to use a seed starter cube. A cube the size of one and a half inch will fit perfectly in a two-inch net pot. These small cubes can hold water while air can reach the roots, which is the most important while germinating seeds.

First, you need to soak your grow cubes in chlorine or chloramine free water with a pH of 5.5. Water from your tap will be around 7-8 pH. You most likely need to use a pH down solution.

Getting the chlorine out of your tap water is quite easy. Let it sit for one day for the chlorine to evaporate. If you want it to evaporate faster, you can use an air stone to air the chlorine out much quicker.

If your water company uses chloramine, you need a reverse osmosis filter to remove the chloramine. Note that not every reverse osmosis filter can remove chloramine. Chloramine can't be aired out and needs to be filtered. If you do not have a reverse osmosis filter available, you can use one thousand mg (one gram) of vitamin C (ascorbic acid) per forty gallons (one hundred and fifty liters) of water.

Use a tray to soak the cubes, pour the water on top, and let it sit for a few minutes. Once most of the water is absorbed, you need to drain the rest of the water. Do not squeeze the cubes. This will remove air pockets inside the cubes.

The following step is dropping your seeds into the holes. This can be a big task if you need to do a lot of seeds. Commercial growers use pelleted seeds and a vacuum seeder to speed this process up. Pelleted seed is a seed that is wrapped in clay. it is bigger, thus easier to handle. You could also use a toothpick and dip the tip in some water. This will make the seed stick to the toothpick, as shown in the following image.

If the holes of the grow media are preventing you from dropping the seed in, use a pen or a toothpick to open the hole back up.

You can use more than one seed per hole if the germination rate is bad. I always use two seeds per hole. When both seeds germinate, I keep the best one and use scissors to remove the bad one.

Place your humidity dome on top of the tray to keep the seed starter cubes moist. Generally, the seeds don't need water until they have germinated. If you notice that your seed starter cubes are drying out, you can pour some more water in the tray. Don't forget to drain the rest of the water.

Rockwool cubes with seedling -Image from bootstrap farmer

Once the seeds start showing its first two leaves, you need to put it under a light source. This will provide the plant with the energy they need to grow. If you experience that the stems are growing long (stretching). It means that your plant is reaching for light. Increase the light on the seedlings to avoid this stretching. Do not use red light on seedlings. White fluorescents that are 6500K are perfect.

After ten days, you can transplant them to your system. If you are growing in a greenhouse, it can take fifteen days in winter.

Heat mats will increase germination during colder weather. The mats are placed under the seedling tray to warm up the seed starting cubes. Setting the heat mat to 68°F is recommended.

Recap:

1. Soak your seed starting cubes in chlorine or chloramine free water. Distilled water is even better. Make sure the pH is around 5.5.
2. Put the seed starting cubes in a tray.
3. Put the seed in the holes of the seed starter cubes.
4. Cover the seed starting cubes with a humidity dome.
5. Set the heat mat to 68°F (20°C) and place it under the tray.
6. Once sprouts appear, water them from the bottom with one quarter nutrient strength. The cubes will wick up the water.
7. Place them under T5 fluorescent lights. The humidity dome is still on the tray.
8. When you see four leaves and the roots are developing out of the seed starting cubes, it is time to transplant them to your growing system.

Nutrients during seedling

Seeds don't need nutrients initially as they are self-contained. However, you can give them a quarter-strength solution, compared to what you are using in your adult plant hydroponic system.

Chapter 10: Choosing Growing Media, Nutrients and Light

Different types of growing media for hydroponics

Media originating from rock or stone

•Perlite

Perlite is produced from volcanic rocks heated to extreme temperatures and then erupts like popcorn, resulting in a clear, porous medium. It has existed longer than any other hydroponic medium. Perlite has excellent oxygen retention, made of air-puffed glass pellets and almost as light as air.

The main reason why it is used as a soil and soil-free mixtures substitute is its ability to retain oxygen. Perlite can be used loose forms, in pots or in slim plastics sleeves, called "growing bags" because the plants are grown right in the bags. Plants are usually installed using a drip feed system in perlite grow bags. Perlite grow bags tend to hold three or four long-term plants.

Perlite's biggest disadvantage is its lightweight consistency, making washing away easy. This disadvantage makes perlite an inappropriate medium in hydroponic systems of flood and flush type or those that would be subjected to strong winds and rains if located outside.

•Rockwool

Rockwool is a molten rock derivative. It is also heated to high temperatures, but then spun into thin, insulation-like fibers. Such fibers are then compressed into cubes and slabs for hydroponic growth or sold loose as "flocks." The cubes are widely used for plant propagation, and slabs are used similarly as perlite growing bags. On the Rockwool slab, a plant is put and grown there.

The roots of the seed grow into the slab. Usually, Rockwool slabs hold three or four long-term plants. Rockwool has long been used as an alternative to fiberglass in building insulation and has been a pillar of commercial hydroponics for the past 20 years. It absorbs water readily and has solid drainage properties, which is why it is commonly used as a seed starting medium and a root cutting medium.

•Lightweight Expanded Clay Aggregate (LECA)

LECA is a very coarse growing medium. Geolite, Grorox, and Hydroton are some of its common trade names. LECA consists of enlarged clay pellets, which can hold water because of their porosity and surface area.
These media are pH neutral and reusable, making them ideally suited for hydroponic systems. Although lava rocks tend to have some of the same characteristics, they should never be used in hydroponic systems because they change the pH and leave behind a thick residue that can damage different types of equipment.

•Vermiculite

Vermiculite is a mineral that expands due to inter-laminary heat when exposed to high temperatures. It is rarely used alone; it is usually combined with other growth materials, especially Perlite. Vermiculite is a good medium because it allows the retention of water, moisture, and nutrients.

•Gravels

Gravel is much the same as sand, with differences in particle size only. The particles of gravel are generally 2 to 15 mm in diameter, while the particles of sand are smaller but still gritty. Sand is more likely to hold water than gravel.

Organic media

•Sawdust

Sawdust was commonly used in industrial hydroponics in British Columbia and Canada, primarily due to its quality. Before use, hardwood sawdusts (e.g. eucalyptus) should be composted. You should never use some softwood sawdusts because they contain highly toxic chemicals. For short-term growth without composting (e.g. for propagation but not for growing a six-month crop), Pinusradiata sawdust was successful.

•Coir fiber (coconut fiber)

Coir fiber has been graciously accepted as a hydroponic growing medium of high quality and is available as a thin, granular substance in several propagation cubes, blocks, Rockwool-like slabs. When used as a growing medium, coir fines should be combined with longer fibers, while fines alone are suitable for raising seeds.
Coir has a high capacity for moisture-holding and air-filled porosity and has a long-term structure. It can be used for several years as a growing medium and sterilized between crops. Some coir supplies that may be contaminated with high sodium levels should be taken good care of. To avoid this problem, hydroponic growers should always choose' sodium-free' horticultural grade coir.

•Composted bark

The use of composted bark has become popular as a peat substitute, providing an excellent seed germination medium as well as hydroponic substrates. In many cases, the bark is preferable to peat if the right grade is chosen.
Nutrient solution for your hydroponic system
Without nutrients, your plants will die. It is that simple. So, your nutrient solution is the key to getting the entire system going. We touched on the simplicity of basic nutrition trumping everything else but let's go into that in more detail. Your solution can usually be broken down into two stages – growth and flower. On top of these you can find additives to tackle different nutrient deficiencies based on the different plants you may be growing. While budget may come into it choosing the most expensive additives isn't a guarantee of good nutrition.

Root Stimulants

These are an essential for hydroponics. Without these you cannot get cuttings to root. These will improve the size and growth rate of your plant's roots so that they can better take up nutrients. Your plant needs the roots as a structural support as well, without strong roots it can't stand up properly or support fruit. Spindly, sickly plants are not productive because they are diverting nutrients to structure rather than leaves, blooms or fruit. Root stimulants are also useful if your plants have root rot as this can help grow new roots before it becomes a problem and the plant loses its means of taking up nutrition. This is an area where price often means performance and is essential for propagating cuttings and in the first stages of your plant's life.

Bloom Maximizers & Vitamins

These are additives that are high in phosphorus and potassium. These should be added on top of your base nutrient because the plant is using more of these specific elements to produce flowers. They are one of the most expensive additives and can be extremely strong. If they're not diluted properly there's a very high chance your plant will suffer nutrient burn, however, they're also very effective at doing what they say. If you're harvesting for the flowers or you want extra flowers, start feeding as your plant shows signs of budding for best results and continue until flowering has finished.
You'll also find that certain vitamins like B1 which works as a boost to the plant's immune system and prevents disease. It can also strengthen the roots against root rot and help prevent shock during the cloning process. It is essential to strong vegetative growth and helps to produce the plant's essential oils and distribution of phosphorous inside the plant cells. It helps plants at all stages of their life cycle which is why it is an important additive. B1 is also known as Thiamine and there's no specific type that's better for your system as long as it is hydroponic compatible, it is also a fairly cheap additive so worth considering.

Bacteria & Enzymes

As part of the plant cycle the roots need bacteria to be able to absorb certain nutrients. These solutions contain a fungus Mycorrhizae which attaches to the roots and exchanges the plant sugars there for nutrients. Adding this to the solution helps improve plant uptake as they are the natural bacterial found in soil. You'll want a Mycorrhizae solution specifically designed for hydroponics. These are especially useful when starting a new crop or propagating because the system will be unlikely to have the necessary bacteria for good uptake.

You can also find enzyme solutions in the same area. Enzymes are active components in your system which break down some of the larger macro nutrients into a smaller molecular form which plants can absorb better. They're also useful for preventing algae and can help plants absorb starches better which makes for a higher sugar content in fruit. Both enzymes and bacteria can be added into your nutrient at any time in your plant life cycle, they're just an essential at the beginning and shouldn't be skimped on.

Sweetener

This is only a necessity for fruiting plants and you only need this during the flower and fruit stage. This is an extra fuel boost for your plants and can enhance the flavor. Basically, sugars fuel the microbes at the roots and to improve sugar content in the plant itself. These also contain a selection of amino acids which are proteins used to build the fiber of the fruits. It is a mix of complex and simple carbohydrates at the core but depending on the type you may also see flavor enhancers which are specific to certain plants. For example, some extremely high carb sweeteners are aimed specifically at tomatoes because of the nutrients added.

Flushing

Before you harvest your plant, you want to clear out the excess solutions and chemicals from it. This means you want to stop using nutrients and solutions about 4-7 days before you plan on harvesting. Flushing agents help remove the bitter chemical taste that can get left behind from heavy metals in the nutrient salts. These build up over time and will ruin the taste of your produce if flushing is not done. Flushing agents help clear these out better than water alone and faster. It restores the plants homeostasis and is essential for food crops. This should only be used in the final stage of growing right before harvesting.

Hydroponics lightening system

They improve the growth of the plants; you need to have the best growing lights. This must be stated that even if fluorescent lights could give light and replace the natural lights that plants get from the sun yet, it cannot provide the necessary spectrum that is needed by the plants.
Their high-pressure lights such as the sodium lights can produce light that covers the red to orange spectrum. They also last longer, and they have a lot of burning energy than the metal halide. They also use reduced energy to perform this function. However, the spectrum of light produced by this light source is quite narrow.

To get the best results, it is advised that you combine the different types of lights to get the results that are close to sunlight just as the spectrum of the sun. You can also cover an ample space with few lights using a light reflector.

Timers

Timers can be used to control lighting, the plants are affected by your lightning and so the timer is of great essence as it helps to remind you when to turn on and off your light, a timer also tells you when to turn on and off your ventilation. A timer also controls the nutrient flow intervals in your Hydroponic garden.

Ballast

This refers to the artificial lighting that is need in Hydroponics. The Ballasd is a component of systems that regulates the voltage that each individual grow light receives. Ballast are usually Electronic, digital or magnetic.
Electronic ballasts do not use Wire and steel core, rather they rely on electro components to regulate the voltage received by a bulb. On the other hand, Magnetic ballasts use Electromagnetic system to regulate the amount of voltage a light bulb receives. The digital ballast is the most efficient of all as it integrates the latest computer technology which makes it smaller and better than the others.

Chapter 11: Diseases & Pests in Hydroponic Systems

Common Diseases and How to Prevent Them

• Algae

This usually grows on the growing media of the plant but can start to creep up on the plant itself. It is a thick green colored gooey mess. Although not a great threat, it is still an indication that there is something not right with your growing environment.
Clean out all vents, change growing media and clean pumps, filters, etc. Change the reservoir water.

• Damping Off

This disease mainly affects seedlings where their growing media is far to damp. Damping off is fatal to the new plant and there is no way to cure it. Once it has attacked the seedling the plant will die. The root of the infected seedling looks like it is waterlogged.
You can prevent the disease by making sure that the media used to house the seedlings is fast draining and sterile. Make sure the seedling cubes are not kept too moist and they are properly drained.

• Downy Mildew

This is not to get confused with powdery mildew. It is a white substance that appears on the upper surface of the leaf, making it look like it has been burned by a cigarette.
Mildew is caused by damp conditions from the humidity in a growing area especially an indoor one. It can usually be wiped away, although it is best to get a non-toxic cleanser from a local nursery to clean the spores away. To discourage mildew, clean away dead leaves, old flowers, produce, etc.

• Gray Mold

This looks like fine cobwebs or silvery hair that usually extends from the leaves of the plant. It is quite common on tomatoes and is caused by too much humidity. Gray mold is not an outbreak you want, once it takes hold it can be quite devastating to the growing environments. and should be caught as early as possible.
Wipe away all the mold that can be found with a soft cloth, making sure to remove every bit of it. Remove all fallen leaves, old flowers, discolored leaves, etc. Each plant in the grow room will have to be thoroughly checked to ensure there is no mold on it.
The entire grow room should be thoroughly cleaned. The humidity in the room will need to be decreased and the air inflow increased.

• Powdery Mildew

Powdery mildew looks just like it sounds as if spots of powder have been dropped on the plant's leaves.
It is caused by high humidity, dampness, and not enough light.
The way to treat it is to decrease the humidity, increase the air circulation in the room and clear off the infected leaves. Make sure there is enough lighting for the plants. If there is too much, a fungicide may have to be considered.

• Wilts

Wilts affect plants like tomatoes, eggplants, and peppers. It causes small spots on the plant's leaves which eventually makes them start to curl up and dry out.
You will notice the leaves of the produce have browned, hardened, curled and dried out.
The only way to cure this disease is to get rid of the infected plants and completely flush out the hydroponic growing environment. Clean out all the dead plants and any debris around the room.

Pests prevention in hydroponic systems

The most famous nuisance problems in hydroponics
In case you want to control sporadically, you first will need to understand that which you might be handling. Listed below are a Part of the nuisances which you're destined to find on the off Possibility that you have bugs on your frame:

Aphids

A lot of people know about aphids from college exercises, also here you thought you're finished together. Be as it might, they really do hydroponic frameworks, especially when your crops have an inordinate quantity of nitrogen within their nutrition supply. They are usually found round the plant stalks and these little people can be dark, green, or grayish/tan.

Whiteflies

Whiteflies may be suspicious; however, you can place them Pretty efficiently. They look like little white moths (approximately 1mm long) and fly off when you are likely to receive you.

Creepy crawly Mites

Creepy crawly vermin are littler than Whiteflies, at below 1mm long. Additional they're definitely among the most feared pervasions of a semi permeable frame. They do seem like slight creepy crawlies, nevertheless since they are so modest, they could without much stretch passing see before an invasion will get far mad.

Organism Gnats

Organism gnats are just another precarious vermin, because the developed gnat is not dangerous, yet the hatchlings is still. You will find the insect hatchlings ingestion at origins, which may expedite bacterial infections until long.

Thrips

Thrips, like aphids, can turn leaves yellowish or Darker considering how they suck on the nutrition's out. They are marginally more affordable at 5mm, however at precisely the exact same time hard to see. They will look like small, dark stains on the upper sides of leaves.

The first stage in hydroponic pest management

Vermin control may be something that you begin rehearsing within the start along with your hydroponic frame. Basically, putting in steps that discourage bugs will be your primary line of shield. Here are the Most Perfect approaches to prevent a vermin problem:

See your stickiness

A couple of bothers, like creepy crawly parasites along with organism gnats, are especially pulled into reduced stickiness and overabundance dampness in various pieces of your frame. Shielding your own stickiness from becoming overly low (half will be an adequate amount to maintain plants seem and ward off insects), can prevent a pervasion. However, it is not about your surrounding condition. Maintaining an inordinate quantity of dampness from the growing moderate can interfere bothers, very similar to expansion gnats, from consuming habitation (especially in the event you use rock wool (they adore).

Step-by-step directions to recognize that a vermin issue

Really, despite stubborn expectation, you can in fact any instance has a hassle slip its way in your frame. Like every hydroponic setup, you need to study your crops for problems consistently. Having said that, you'd prefer to not confuse signs of germs with signs of distinct issues, as an instance, supplement inadequacy or illness. Here is the way to inform if your crops are undergoing germs, or another illness:

Staining

At the stage when discomforts drain the nutritional supplements from leaves (such as aphids do), you will understand that the leaves become stained and often turn a yellowish shading. This discoloration is sprinkled around minor openings the vermin feed out of, not only for the most part distribute on leaves.

Spots

A couple of bugs may leave a mark illustration of stains, Irrespective of whether yellow, white, dark colored, or dim. On the off probability that you view places, confirm whether they are shops on the leaves (out of eggs, defecation, etc.), or real injury to those leaves. On the off probability that the stains scratch, you can all around bet you own a bug problem. At the stage when you find those on almost any plant, assess the leaves and stalks of distinct plants to determine the aggravation and the amount of intrusion.

Gaps from insects versus absorbs and sores

At the stage once you initially see a difference or rip, it will be anything but hard to create feelings. That's the reason it is crucial to watch closer and look at the advantages of some openings. Copies should be self-evident, since they will appear where warmth and light sources are close crops and reveal staining round any openings or absorbs.
The bugs which Are well on how to frighten hydroponic nurseries are far more 'suckers' compared to 'munchers.' That suggests that the openings that they depart from profiting from crops are small, and frequently raised and surrounded by an increasingly yellowish, or whitish land.

Things to do when you've got vermin?

On the off probability that you have seen a part of this above unwanted effects of a vermin problem, you must get it repaired as well as rapidly. Lamentably as soon as an aggravation has progressed in, it may be tough to relieve the matter. Nuisances can undergo a hydroponic framework for an astonishing speed, therefore once 1 plant has been affected others will generally follow quite soon.

Chapter 12: Pesticides & Treatments in Hydroponics

How to treat your ill plants

Diseases are awful whether we're talking about humans or about our plants. Here we will look at the most common diseases that hydroponic growers find themselves facing.
Iron Deficiency

You can recognize the iron deficiency in plants from the so-called leaf chlorosis: the leaves of the plant turn yellow while the veins of the leaves stay green.

To diagnose an iron deficiency, you want to test your growing operation. Do a pH test and check the numbers. Higher than 7.0 can cause many plants to stop absorbing iron. Also, do an EC reading and check your levels; you may have an imbalance. Remember that an EC check doesn't confirm how many of each nutrient is in your solution so you may consider changing out the nutrient solution for a freshly balanced batch.

If you have identified an iron deficiency, the first thing you should do is fix the pH and EC levels and get that all within the proper range. You can also buy liquid iron which you use to spray down your plants. Spray the liquid iron directly on the leaves. Liquid iron is only a quick fix and not the solution, so if it shows results then consider tweaking your nutrient solution to include more iron.

Powdery Mildew

To deal with powdery mildew, you want to prune away some of the plant to open it up to better airflow. This will help to reduce the humidity of the plant to make it less inviting to powdery mildew. Remove any foliage that is already infected and make sure to clean up any fallen plant matter. A spray made of 60% water and 40% milk can be used once every two weeks to help prevent powdery mildew from taking hold. Also wash your plants from time to time, as this will help prevent both powdery mildew and a variety of pests. A fungicide can be applied if the problem is extreme but this also risks hurting the plants.

Gray Mold

Gray mold likes to settle in near the bottom of the plant and in the areas that the plant shadows the most. It tends to begin on flowers that have wilted and then it quickly spreads out to the leaves and stem. It really likes those areas with a high humidity. The infected plants will begin to rot away and if left untreated, gray mold is one of the most disgusting diseases to have to deal with. The spores like cool temperatures and high humidity and they can get into the healthy tissue of the plants directly so your plants are especially susceptible after a trimming.

Pruning your plants or setting up on with a trellis helps to improve the air circulation and lower the humidity of your plants so that gray mold will desire them less. You can also use a small fan to increase the airflow around your plants. Always remove any fallen plant matter. If you spray your plants down in the morning, give them time to dry so that gray mold is less interested in the bed. Fungicides can also help in tackling gray mold infections.

Preventing Diseases

The most important thing we can do to help our plants avoid becoming diseased is to make sure that they are healthy and not overly stressed. This means we want to check our pH and EC levels regularly to make sure that they are in the proper range. We also want to make sure that we clean our reservoir from time to time and have a schedule for cycling out the old solution and filling it back up with a new, freshly balanced one. This will help your plants to stay healthy which helps them to fend off attacks by pathogens.

You also want to keep your garden as clean as possible. Like with pests, using a two-door airlock system will give you an area in which to wipe down and clean up before you enter the garden. Doing this helps to remove dirt from your person, which is absolutely the leading way for pathogens to get introduced into your setup. Make sure to clean your hands and any tools you plan to use in the garden before you start messing around. Also, clean off your boots and consider removing any jacket or outdoor wear that you have on.

Clean up any spills as soon as they happen to avoid introducing extra moisture and humidity around your plants as these attract disease. Also make sure that you are removing any dead plant matter as soon as you spot it. Dead plant matter becomes a breeding ground for both pests and disease. Check your plants for disease regularly and remove any that show signs of heavy infection. Consider washing your plants down twice a week or so to knock off any pests or infection that may be trying to take hold.

By keeping vigilant and maintaining your garden, you can prevent disease from taking hold and ensure that you are raising healthy, beautiful crops.

Organic pesticides & treatments

Preventing Pests

Now that we have an idea of the pests that are most common to hydroponic gardens, let us turn our attention towards how we prevent these pests from getting into our gardens in the first place. Many of these techniques will help us to identify a possible infestation as it is trying to get started and so they offer us early warnings to prepare ourselves to battle pests. If we keep up our preventative measures and keep our eyes peeled for pests, then we can save our plants a lot of damage and ourselves a lot of time by cutting off the problem at the head.

When it comes to pests it is also important to understand that not every pest is the same. This doesn't just mean that whiteflies are different from fungus gnats. What this means is that fungus gnats on the West coast are going to be different than fungus gnats on the East coast. Not every solution for prevention or extermination will work. A certain pesticide may be used to kill gnats on the East but the ones on the West might have grown an immunity to it. For this reason, it is important to check with your local hydroponics store to see if there is any region-specific information you need to tackle your pest problem.

One of the ways that we prevent pests is to make sure that we limit their ability to enter our garden in the first place. We can do this in a few ways. Insect screens go a long way to keeping out pests. We also want to limit the amount of traffic in and around our setups. If possible, our setups will benefit greatly if they can be protected by airlock entrances as these offer the most secure protection against both pests and pathogens. Airlocks can be doubled up to create a space before the garden in which to wipe down dirt and any insects or eggs that are catching a free ride on your clothing.

In order to see if pests are starting to show up in your garden, use sticky traps around your plants. Yellow and blue sticky traps are both useful, as they attract different pests, so you want to make sure to use both kinds for the best results. Place traps near any entrances into your gardens such as doors or ventilation systems. Also, make sure to place one or two near the stems of your plants to catch those pests that prefer snacking on the lower bits, such as aphids or fungus gnats. Get into the habit of checking these traps regularly as they can give you a great idea of what kind of life is calling your garden home.

While traps will help us to get a head start fighting any infections, they aren't a foolproof method when it comes to avoiding pests. Traps should be used together with personal spot checks. This means that you should be checking your plants for pests a couple of times a week. Take a clean cloth and check the bottom of your leaves. Check around the roots for any fungus gnat larvae. You can check the tops of leaves visually. Look for any signs of yellowing or bite marks as described above.

Make sure to remove any weeds that take up root in your garden as these plants are only going to sap your garden's resources and offer a breeding ground for pests. Also remove dead or fallen plant matter, of course. This includes leaves but also any fruit, buds or petals that have been dropped.

Finally, before you introduce any new plants to your garden, make sure to quarantine them first so that you can check them for pests. You can use a magnifying glass to get a closer look if you need to. Give the new plants a thorough inspection, making sure to check all parts of the plant and the potting soil before you transfer it over.

By creating a system and a schedule for inspecting your plants, you can prevent an infestation of pests from ruining your garden or causing you a lot of headaches. A vigilant eye will give you the upper hand in both preventing and dealing with any kind of problem you have with pests. Remember, a strong defense is the best offense when it comes to keeping your plants healthy and free from harm.

Chapter 13: Choosing the Best Lighting Medium for Your Hydroponic Plants

To upgrade the development of your plants, you must acquire lights. It is critical to refer now that even though glaring lights can be utilized to enhance characteristic light, they can't, all alone, give the range of light required by plants.

Metal Halide and High-Pressure Sodium Lights were created to discharge a range of light that impersonates the nature of light radiating from the sun. Metal Halide lights are the nearest you can get to daylight. They produce progressively a higher extent of blue light that is incredible for supporting vegetative development.

High weight sodium lights then again produce light that spreads a greater amount of the red-orange range. They last more, consume more splendid and expend a lower measure of vitality than their metal halide partners, even though they produce a smaller range of light. For the best outcomes, it is suggested that you join the utilization of the two kinds of lights to give light that is as close as conceivable to the full range of daylight. Moreover, you can utilize light reflectors and movers to cover a more extensive space with less lights.

Fake lighting techniques

Sorts of Grow Lights

There are three essential sorts of develop lights accessible for indoor urban cultivating: Fluorescent develop lights, HPS or HID develop lights, and LED develop lights.

1. **Fluorescent Grow Lights**. Fluorescent develop lights are utilized for developing herbs and vegetables inside. They are two sorts, including fluorescent cylinders and Compact Fluorescent Lights (CFLs). Fluorescent cylinders come in a wide range of forces. They last more and are more vitality productive than glowing bulbs- - the normal bulbs that have been lighting homes for quite a long time. Bright light bulbs are flimsy and can without much of a stretch fit into little spaces. With respect to drawbacks, they require a weight to direct present and the cylinders require a stand, instead of a traditional attachment.

Such necessities can add to the expense of establishment.

Then again, CFLs have turned out to be progressively basic in family use and not simply in indoor urban cultivating. CFLs utilize just 20 to 30% of the vitality devoured by customary brilliant bulbs and their life expectancy is six to multiple times longer. They are by a long shot the least expensive among every one of the three significant sorts of develop lights. One outstanding favorable position with CFL bulbs is they don't emanate abundance heat, enabling ranchers to keep the lights nearer to the plants. This low warmth highlight makes it very vitality effective too.

2. **HPS Grow Lights**: High-Pressure Sodium (HPS) lights have developed in prominence and are surpassing fluorescent cylinders and bulbs. These lights are progressively normal among business and experienced indoor cultivators and the innovation behind them is settled, effectively more than 75 years of age.

The issue with HPS is that it delivers a lot of warmth. All things considered, you should keep the lights a decent good way from the plants. They require a lot of venture to set up and keep up. Subsequently, HPS isn't suggested for little producers.

3. **Driven Grow Lights**: While the beginnings of LED innovation initially rose in the mid 1900s, the red and blue LEDs ideal for indoor cultivating started being utilized only preceding the 2000s.

Driven develop lights are the most vitality proficient among each of the three essential kinds of develop lights. These sources can be put more distant from plants while yet delivering enough light without expending a lot of vitality. CFLs are practically half less proficient than LED develop lights. The warmth generation by LED develop lights is almost zero. Above all, LED performs best to make an ideal indoor condition to make practically any sort of nourishment.

The expense of LED lights is higher than other two sorts, be that as it may. Also, laborers working in indoor ranches need to utilize eye insurance as LEDs can be unsafe to human eyes.

Characteristics of lighting techniques

The most straightforward approach to arrangement fake lighting for an indoor nursery is to recollect these dependable guidelines. 40 watts for each square foot for high light plants like tomatoes and peppers and 25 watts for every square foot for low light plants like lettuce and verdant plants.

This implies for an average 4' x 4' space, you would require 400 watts of lighting to develop low light adoring plants, and 600 watts of lighting to develop high return plants like huge tomato and pepper plants.

Joining Natural and Artificial Lighting Techniques

When thought about two unmistakable ways of thinking in agriculture, the line among indoor and open-air development is being obscured. Profoundly complex, all year nurseries are at the front line of this combination development as they use the accepted procedures of the two strategies in an innovative give and take. These tasks use the sun's vitality to control basic plant capacities while actualizing indoor developing advancements like light sensors, power outage covering frameworks, dehumidifiers, and mechanical radiators to mirror indoor ecological controls in open air settings.

Supplemental Lighting

Maybe the most essential innovative application in these current nurseries is that of supplemental lighting. In indoor planting, lighting is one of the most significant elements directing the result of a gather. Be that as it may, it is additionally perhaps the costliest component of an activity, with an overhead of in any event $400 per unit for 1,000W twofold finished high weight sodium (HPS) lights and $800 per unit for similar light emanating diodes (LEDs). Taken to a business scale, this overhead can demonstrate very scary as it is exclusively dependent on these counterfeit light sources to nourish each square inch of a gigantic nursery overhang. At that point there is the galactic expense of running the lights in these huge scale set-ups. Some 10,000-square-foot distribution center develops have detailed power bills as much as $12,000 month to month.

Nonetheless, current nurseries utilize best practices from both indoor and outside development. With regards to lighting, this implies using a cautious parity of daylight and supplemental light. It is changing the way in which individuals develop crops outside.

Here are a few hints on the best way to capitalize on your new develop room.

#1. Picking the Perfect Measure of Room for Your Plants

The main thing to remember before you set up your develop room: the amount you will develop. When you have a smart thought of what number of plants will consume the indoor develop room, you can decide how a lot of room you must leave between the plants and the light source you will require.

#2. Finding the Correct Gear

By using the correct gear in your develop room configuration can positively be the contrast among progress and disappointment.

Using the right LED lights will help since the innovation in them is at long last making up for lost time to the lights most expert cultivators have utilized for quite a long time. Likewise make certain to have a period change to consequently kill the lights on and for when your plants explicitly need it.

Your cannabis develop room can't flourish without ventilation. With no moving air, the plants will overheat and kick the bucket. It is ideal to utilize a wind stream framework and a fan for predictable air course so the temperature and carbon dioxide will spread equitably all through the room.

At long last, a waterproof floor is significant in your development room arrangement and configuration just as an approach to check the stickiness. Having the appropriate measure of dampness noticeable all around will help the development of your plants, and yet guarantee there isn't an excessive amount of stickiness, which will avoid organism and form development. If you need to go down the hydroponic way, it will diminish the requirement for pesticides and herbicides. Likewise, hydroponically developed plants become quicker and can lessen water utilization by up to 90% rather than ordinary agrarian strategies.

#3. Give Appropriate Supplements to Your Plants

When planning a develop room, make certain to utilize living or natural soil in your pots. As indicated by Cannabis and Tech Today, "Living soil is wealthy in microorganisms and microfauna, which separate supplements in the dirt and make them simpler for the plant to retain. Natural soils and supplements are not just economical, plants developed with these strategies will in general have a stronger taste and flavor profiles than buds developed by using non-natural techniques."

Simply recollect that it will be critical to give nitrogen, potassium, and phosphorus for your plants, however don't try too hard. Nitrogen lethality is excessively regular of a ruin for producers.

#4. Guarantee Your Plants are Sheltered and Secure

It ought to abandon saying that you won't be a fruitful cannabis rancher if your plants are devastated or demolished. When you investigate your develop room arrangement and configuration, are there enough bolts for the entryways? Are there in any case somebody could vandalize the area? It may likewise be ideal to think about putting resources into cameras. It is an additional expense, yet it could wind up sparing you a great deal of cash contrasted with having your plants taken or devastated.

Those are only a couple of proposals on the best way to capitalize on your cannabis develop room. Make certain to take a gander at all the various choices you have and choose what is the best way for you to guarantee the most beneficial and most strong yields conceivable.

Chapter 14: The Beginner's Most Common Mistakes

As a beginner, you are bound to make mistakes. Mistakes happen—there is no real way around that. However, you should keep in mind that mistakes should also not be made from sheer ignorance whenever possible. If you are going to be setting up your own hydroponic system, you are better off acknowledging what the common mistakes are so you can then ensure that you are not repeating them yourself. It is better to be fully informed than unsure of how to protect yourself.

We are going to go over several of the most common mistakes that beginners make when it comes to hydroponic setups. These mistakes are very easily avoidable if you know what you are doing, and you should do everything in your power to do exactly that. If you know better, you can do better!

Not Paying Attention to pH

The pH in your system is perhaps the most levels in your entire system. If you do not pay attention to the pH levels of your system, you will find that your plants suffer. Your plants will need you to make sure that your nutrient solution and to do so, you will need the proper equipment. The best way to do this is to either get a litmus test or to get a pH meter to allow yourself to monitor the pH levels.

If your solution is either too alkaline or too acidic, your plants will either fail to get the proper nutrients, or it will die entirely, and that is a problem. To prevent this, you will want to ensure that your solution is balanced regularly. If you notice that your plants are not doing well, check the pH. If you feel like your system is not working, check the pH. It should be a normal part of your general maintenance.

However, many people feel like they can ignore this step altogether. They may assume that either they do not need to measure because they have chosen a fertilizer that they know will work okay for the plants that they are looking at growing or because they were being lazy or simply did not care.

Cheap Lighting

Cheap lighting is another very common mistake. While you can use less expensive lighting in some respects, some people make the mistake of not making sure that their lighting is good for their system at all. They do not consider the fact that it is possible that the lighting that they are using could very well possibly be meant for something entirely different. It is important to do your research here. Most normal indoor lights will not be enough for most of your plants.

Lighting should always be the biggest investment that you make for your plants. If you are spending big bucks on the lighting, it is oftentimes for a reason. Of course, you will have to stop and double check that the lighting that you are looking at buying is going to be the right kind for you and your current needs.

Too many people assume that they will not need the higher quality lighting for one reason or another, but that is a huge problem—the quality of the lighting matters immensely. When you do not make sure that the lighting is enough, you run the risk of it simply not working at all for your plants.

You must also remember that the windowsill is not enough light for most plants. You will need to double check the needs of your plants, but for the most part, the light in your window will not be enough for anything but those that live in the shade normally.

Improper Nourishing

Many people do not actually spend the time to research the nuances of plant food, especially in the early days. They may buy a big back of fertilizer and think that all they need to do is mix the fertilizer into their water in order to allow for the nourishment to be then passed on to the plants. However, there is a huge problem with doing this—if you simply use the fertilizer meant to go in soil, you may find that you actually just clog everything up instead. You may also find that ultimately, you grab food for all your plants without recognizing the differences between what your plants will need and which stages of growth they are in. It is important to note that the stage of growth is critically important to ensuring the health of your plants by providing them with all of the nutrition that they will require.

Flowering and fruiting plants will need very different nutrition than a plant in a vegetative stage, for example. Your tomatoes will want very different nutrients than your lettuce as well. If you are growing several different plants within one system, you must make sure that you have found a concentration that will work for all the plants in your system, or you run the risk of killing something.

Failing to Sanitize

A common mistake made by beginners is foregoing the sanitization stages. Remember, you are growing food in your system, and you should grow that food with plenty of care given to it. You want to make sure that you are not only sanitizing it regularly, you are also making sure that you keep it clean.

This means that you must remove the plant waste that you pull out. Make sure that it gets composted or properly disposed off, so you do not have it festering in your hydroponic garden. You should also make sure that your floors are kept clean and dry.

You want to ensure that you are regularly sterilizing everything as well. This means that you must sterilize the system itself, the tools, and anything else that will be kept in the room to ensure that it is kept in the proper condition to make use of it when it is needed.

Not Learning When You Have the Chance

Finally, the last mistake that is very common amongst beginners is failing to learn.

You may feel like you already know what you are doing, or you feel like there is no reason to spend time learning how to do it. You may not feel like doing the research, or you think that you know better. This is a problem—your system will fail if you do not maintain it, and to maintain it, you must know what you are doing.

Read something about the subject! Pick up another one! Learn about the plants that you are growing! Make sure that you are spending ample time going through all the information that you will need to know in order to ensure that your garden will be successful. It is not an easy task to garden, but it is one that can take you very far in life if you are able to make regular work of it. All you must do is ensure that you put in the effort while you still can and before you make your system worse off.

Chapter 15: Tips & Tricks

To get the optimum results out of the hydroponic system, you must know the right way of growing hydroponic plants so that they will yield more crops. Many people quickly get disappointed with hydroponic gardening, amateur growth, and as they are beginners. However, the reason for this disappointment can be one of these:

- Lack of ability- for hydroponic system, you need experience, or you don't have enough equipment or supplies.
- 2. Unorganized- you know everything regards to hydroponic gardening, but you want to put forth the maximum effort into it.
- 3. May be lack of knowledge- means you don't have enough experience concerning hydroponic gardening.

Let's put some light on the varied hydroponic tips and tricks in below points by which you can become an expert and fulfill your dreams:

1.Choosing the right type of crop

In the technique of the hydroponic system, almost every plant can grow, but as a beginner, you can start with small plants by which you gain knowledge and experience.
The first step is, choose those plants which need less maintenance and nutrients. As a beginner, you can take herbs and vegetables. Therefore, growing small plants can improve your experience as well as learn new things which are best for the future when you produce other plants.

2.Make a proper plan

When you make up your mind to plant a specific type of crop in your hydroponic garden, the following step comes is planning. Means knowing varied kind of nutrients which are essential for plant, various equipment, photoperiod, etc. so that you have a full overview of how it can offer better results.
Make a list of every small to the massive thing before planting a crop.

3.Why and when to test and adjust the Ph level in hydroponic plants

Every plant which you plant in your hydroponic garden only absorbs nutrient solution in the PH if the answer is in between the range of plant which you have planted. However, if the Ph is not up to the mark, then it won't matter how much your nutrient solution is, the plants will suffer from malnutrition and will die after some time.
If you are a beginner, it is recommended that you check the PH of the plants daily for the best results.

4.Have proper and enough lighting

When you search the market, you will get countless types of grow lights according to your budget.

The types of lighting are:

- High-Intensity Discharge (HID) is suitable for extensive hydroponic gardens that have virtuous airflow and proper ventilation.
- Compact Fluorescent Lights (CFL) offer good results in small rooms.
- Light Emitting Lights (LED) are also best for small hydroponic gardening, but they are more expensive than CFLs.

Any type of light you choose, make sure that it will discharge light between 400 and 700 nanometers.

5.Having control on temperature

This is one of the essential tips of hydroponic gardening. If the temperature of the plant exceeds 85 degrees, the overall growth of the plants will stop quickly. If the gardener is using HID lights, then it becomes challenging to control the temperature.

In order to maintain the accurate temperature, the gardener you must install centrifugal fans, but in some cases, the fans alone cannot solve the problem.

For this, plan hydroponic gardening when the outside temperature is 55 degrees or less. Therefore, it is possible to pull fresh air in the garden. On the other hand, you can install air conditioning.

6.The right type of equipment

First and foremost, one thing which you need to consider before setting up a system of the hydroponic garden is to have proper and unique tools. Like- dark area, hydroponic gardening system, an oscillating fan, TDS meter, maybe an air conditioner, a digital timer, etc.

7.Select an appropriate nutrient

You must gain knowledge of various nutrients, which are crucial for plant growth when you start gardening. Side by side, you must know about the quantity of nutrients required by the different plants you have grown.

8.The health of the roots

The health of the root is essential for the overall growth of the plant. Time to time check the origins of the crop so that plants will not suffer from any damage. While offering nutrients to the plants minimizes the amount of light so that algae and fungus will not damage the roots of the crops.

9.Offering water to the plants

This tip is essential because overwatering the plants will damage the crops. As a matter of fact, the water intake of the plants depends on the type of plants whether they are small or large.

Crops that grow on dry season need more water than crops that grow in a humid climate. On the other hand, some plants hold moisture for a long time as compared to other plants. So, while planting a crop, see whether it needs more water or less so that you can set up the water draining system.

10. Maintain the humidity level

Different plants have a different level of humidity on which they can survive on their development. So, keep in mind that plants will grow faster and yield higher crops when they are given the proper level of humidity.

11. Airflow and ventilation should be proper

For the healthy growth of crops, airflow is a vital part, which also aids in maintaining the overall temperature of the plants. Fans and air conditioners should be installed in appropriate areas so that plants will be healthy.

12. Understand Ph first

The understanding of PH level in plants is must get successful in hydroponic gardening. Interestingly, some meters can take the Ph readings, but on your side, you also must understand this. The main reason for checking the PH level of plants is that water doesn't have a proper range of Ph by which plants can die or suffer from malnutrition.

13. Make liberal use of your pruning shears

Any time of the day when you see something on the plant, just prune it away, it can rot the full plant. The cleaner you keep your plant higher the yield.

14. Think about the taste of the fruits or vegetables

In this regard, which fruit or vegetable tastes excellent when it is purchased from the market or plucked from the hydroponic garden?
The main reason for doing this is there is an end number of crops that don't have a different taste. Either they are purchased from the market or plucked from the garden. Before deciding to choose the crop to plant, give priority to those fruits or vegetables that taste better when they are freshly harvested from the garden.

15. Take care of space and type of hydroponic system

Well, it is fascinating to grow crops such as corns, melons, and squash, etc. but the point is they need wide space. Make sure that you choose the right system and appropriate hydroponic kits. There are countless factors like ventilation, water, etc. are crucial elements that make the hydroponic system successful.

16. Always plant fastest-growing, most natural cultivation, and most crucially which offer high yield

In this field, you have learned as much as you can, depending on your capability. This is the only way by which you can decide which is the right crop for your hydroponic system. Find out the seeds which are cheap and yield high so that your profit margin is also high.

17. Explore vitamins B

Many of the beginners in hydroponic gardening ignore the impact of stress on the plants. If you see that your plants are not suffering from any of the diseases, then also, they can face stress issues. So, if you think that your plants are facing stress issues, offer them vitamin B supplements that are safe, and with that growth will surge significantly.
These above tips are basic ones, especially for beginners who say that hydroponic gardening is complicated.

Chapter 16: Strategies to Avoid Insects

The term pest control often conjures up images of people using sprays filled with chemicals. You might think that using such methods is rather extreme. But if you spot your wonderful tomatoes surrounded by ants or your beautiful flowers suddenly attacked by flies, then you might think of drowning those creatures in pesticides.

However, what might sound like a frightening scenario can typically be solved by taking a few precautionary steps. If all else fails and you still would like to consider using sprays, then do not worry.

The thing about pesticides is that they have an instant (and noticeable) effect. You can see the number of pests on your plants reduced. Nevertheless, there are certain effects in the long term – such as depleting the health of your soil and slightly poisoning your water – that might prove disastrous for you in the future. You might have to change the soil entirely. If you are using a raised bed, then this might not be a problem. However, if you have decided to plant directly into the earth, then getting rid of that entire pesticide residue is a strenuous process.

Here is another thing that you should keep in mind; sometimes, getting rid of the pests may not be necessary. If you have aphids roaming around on your plants, then see if you have helpful insects that dine on these aphids. In fact, certain farmers are known to let the pests live. This is because they usually have some form of predator that can take care of the pest problem. This has two beneficial results:

- You do not have to spend time (and money, in some situations) on pest control activities.
- You let someone (or something) else take care of the problem for you. A friend in need is a friend indeed. Even if that friend just happens to have four legs, wings, or antennae.

Another thing to keep in mind; your problem might not be related to pests. It is easy to think that certain creatures have wreaked havoc on your lovely garden. Actually, it is certainly tempting to think that way. However, in many cases, the situation might just be because of other factors. Is there enough moisture for the plants? Are strong winds causing harm to them? Was there heavy rainfall recently? Did it hail? Even water pollution could be another factor to consider. You see, all these factors cause unnecessary stress on the plants, which further begins to attract the pests in your area. Trying to get to the root of the problem might help you effectively remove the pests without using any pest control techniques (including pesticides).

The idea behind evaluating your garden is to know what kind of problem you are dealing with. That may help you decide if you would like to head over to the following step, which is the integrated pest management, or 'IPM' for short, process.

In IPM, farmers and gardeners take gradually stronger steps to get rid of the pests in their garden. They start by working on the conditions that help the growth of the crops. Are these conditions beneficial? Do the crops have everything they need? Once they can work around these conditions, they seek to establish a level of damage they can accept. Once that is done, they move on to using methods that have minimal toxicity. If that does not work, they begin using toxic or invasive methods.

Join the Resistance!

The first thing that you should do is focus on creating pest resistance plants. You see, gardeners and farmers often work with a plethora of plants species. Some of these plants have some unique traits. One of those unique traits is the ability of the plant to have disease resistance. This means that the plant suffers minimal damage from a specific disease, like how the human immune system builds resistances against diseases.

Many of the modern plants have built resistance to many diseases that could cause considerable damage. What's more, you can find plants that also have resistance to certain insects. For example, you can find special types of squash that can keep away certain types of beetles. This might help you effectively find a solution against these pests without having to resort to other methods of pest control.

In fact, when you are purchasing plants, you might receive information about what pests those plants resist. After knowing what pests are common in your area, you can match the plant to that particular pest.

Inviting Less Pests

While you might be confident that you have taken all the precautionary steps to keep away pests, there might be certain reasons your garden is still attracting those nasty critters.
Mixed Plants
Most insects have receptors that allow them to target their favorite plants. It is how bees can seek out nectar so easily. If you have the plants that insects are waiting to attack and you have done nothing to protect those plants, then you might as well schedule buffet hours for the insects!

What you can do to avoid this situation is to plant your crops in small batches throughout your garden. Then you can add other plants into the mix (preferably those that have resistance against the pests in your area). This confuses the insects, tricking them into believing that perhaps your garden does not have the food they are looking for. Additionally, you might be able to avoid diseases from spreading when you mix plant breeds.

Timing

Certain pests often arrive during certain climates. This fact might give you an idea of the kind of threat you are dealing with. When plants are young, they do not have the strength to ward off pests effectively, which is why you can plant your crops early so that by the time pest climate arrives, your crops have strong tissues. In some cases, insects often leave eggs behind in gardens. When the larvae hatch, they find a ready source of food in the plants around them. For this reason, you could also plant your crops a few weeks after the larvae have hatched, allowing you to starve the pests before working on your garden.

Here is a pro tip: speak to farmers in your area about the emergence of pests. They have extensive knowledge about when these pests might come out during a particular season, allowing you to know how long to wait before planting your crops.

Crop Rotation

You can move around the crops to new locations in your greenhouse each year. This does not give pests a particular spot to target. Shifting locations confuses the pests, who might be used to finding plants in a specific spot of the garden. Certain insects often lay their eggs in one location when they realize that they know where they can find a ready supply of food. However, by moving your crops around, larvae that hatch might not find their food source. Before they can discover food, they might starve and you might be able to get rid of them without much effort. Do note that crop rotation is most commonly possible with annual plants, when they can be cycled year after year.

Go Easy on the Fertilizer

This might be a common mistake for beginners. Gardeners who are starting out might worry about the amount of fertilizer that they use. Many farmers use too much to avoid using too little. Unfortunately, too much fertilizer can cause harm to plants, just the way too little can. In fact, you could say that increasing the amount of fertilizer to a plant is like giving steroids to them! For example, soil nutrients provide nitrogen to the plant. This is good in moderate quantities. By adding more fertilizer, you increase the supply of nitrogen. Providing excess amounts of nitrogen might cause rapid growth in plants. This causes them to end up being juicy. This might not sound all that bad. Who doesn't love juicy food? You and every other multi-legged creature will be waiting to get a bite out of those plants. Pests might become attracted to the unnatural growth, finding a rich source of food for them and their offspring.

Clean Up Other Materials

If you notice fallen leaves, fruits, or other objects in your garden that should not typically be there, then make sure you clear them out. These objects and debris might carry organisms and pests on them that could be transferred to your plants. This increases the chances of infecting your plants with diseases or sending pests into their midst. Once you have cleaned up, see if you can also cultivate the soil when you get the opportunity. This reveals any hidden pest eggs. Additionally, if there are any larvae, you might just let predators (or even the weather) get rid of them.

Make Friends with Creatures

I am not asking you to invite creatures into your house for tea and supper. What I mean is to allow the growth of certain organisms that could help you get rid of pests. For example, certain types of spiders leave your plants alone, but find abundant food in the pests that might live there. You can always encourage the growth of these pest-hunters, as you can call them.

Insecticides

These are a form of pesticide that are specifically made to harm, eliminate, or repel one or more species of insect. You can discover insecticides in various forms such as sprays, gels, and even traps. Pick one based on the pest that is attacking your garden.
Once you have selected your insecticide, it is better to know the below tips:
- I would recommend using just one type of insecticide in your garden. Adding two or more insecticides diminishes their effect and may inadvertently cause harm to your garden.
- Remember that not all insecticides take the same time to remove pests from your garden. You might have to wait longer for certain types to work.
- Try to see if you really need the spray. For example, if you want to get rid of ants, you could use a bait instead (after all, ants are attracted to nearby sources of food).

Fungicides

These are pesticides that are made to kill fungal infections on the plants and any fungi spores that might have latched onto your crops. In some cases, fungicides are used to mitigate the effects of mildew and mold. The way they function is by damaging either the fungal cell structure or stopping the energy production in cells.

Chapter 17: Hydroponic System Maintenance

Now, we will go into how you can maintain the water-nutrient solution, pH balance, and cleanliness of your hydroponic system. All three of these aspects are incredibly important as if any of them aren't maintained, your plants will become stunted or even die off from disease or malabsorption.

Water-Nutrition Solution

In hydroponics, instead of having the nutrients in the soil, you add it to the water. You can buy hydroponic-specific fertilizers that are either liquid or dry, organic, or inorganic. These fertilizers allow you to add the exact amount of nutrients a given plant needs to the water. This increases the growth of the vegetation, as the roots don't have to search through soil for their needed nutrients.

There are multiple macronutrient plants require to maintain a healthy and balanced life cycle. But, the most important are N, P, and K. Still, it is important to understand all their macronutrient needs, so let's look at them in turn.

Nitrogen (N)

Often considered the most important nutrient, nitrogen is responsible for vegetative growth and color. Nitrogen also allows a plant to produce necessary proteins, amino acids, enzymes, and chlorophyll. All these elements work together to allow a plant to grow bigger and healthier. For this reason, people usually use a fertilizer that prioritizes nitrogen for the growth period of a plant before the plant begins flowering or bearing fruits or vegetables.

If a plant is lacking enough nitrogen, they will begin to develop yellow leaves. You will first notice this yellowing in the older and lower leaves on a plant, which will drop off and die before long.

On the other hand, it is difficult to notice if your plants are getting too much nitrogen. When this happens, your plants may be vibrant and healthy, but they will struggle to bear fruits and vegetables or bloom. This is because the plant will spend all its energy on growing bigger, rather than producing flowers or fruit.

Phosphorus (P)

Just as nitrogen is incredibly important, so too is phosphorus. This nutrient is the main component of the DNA of plants, which plays a role in the development of roots, fruit/vegetables, flowers, and seeds.

This nutrient is important for the entire stage of a plant's life. But it is especially important during the germination, seedling, and flowering stages. If your plant doesn't have enough phosphorus, it will be shown in weaker or shorter growth in the roots, leaves, and flowers. But you also don't want to give a plant too much phosphorus. If a plant has too much of this nutrient, it will prevent it from absorbing other important nutrients such as iron, calcium, copper, magnesium, and zinc.

Potassium (K)

Required in large amounts for early plant development and reproduction, potassium is another macronutrient found in fertilizer. But it is different than the other nutrients in one big way—it doesn't form plant-based compounds. Instead, potassium is used for the processes of photosynthesis and protein synthesis, as well as the formation of starch and activation of enzymes.
Similarly to nitrogen, if your plants are low in potassium, they will reveal it by yellowing of the leaves. And, similarly to phosphorus, if they have too much potassium, they will be unable to absorb certain nutrients. In this case, they will struggle to utilize iron, zinc, and magnesium.

Calcium

Important for the development and formation of cells, calcium is another important macronutrient. It is often revealed when a plant has too little access to calcium when the edges and tips of leaves turn brown and die. When plants are early in the growth phase, too much calcium can stunt plant growth.

Sulfur

This macronutrient is a component of the twenty-one amino acids found in plants that are used to create protein. Not only that, but it is also used to form and activate certain vitamins and enzymes.

Magnesium

This mineral is one of the main components that is used to produced chlorophyll. When a plant undergoes the photosynthesis process, it is magnesium that helps it to create oxygen. This is especially used in large numbers in fast-growing plants and those with a lot of vegetative growth.

Now that we have gone over the macronutrients, it is time to look at the micronutrients. Plants may need these nutrients in a smaller number, but don't underestimate their importance.

Zinc

Another nutrient important to produce chlorophyll, zinc is also used in the process or metabolizing nitrogen.

Iron

Many people are familiar with this mineral, as humans require it just as much as plants do. Iron is important for photosynthesis, the formation of chlorophyll, nitrogen fixation, and energy provision.

Manganese

This mineral is used to create oxygen during the photosynthesis process and catalyze the growth process.

Boron

Lastly, boron is used alongside calcium to build the structure and maintain the function of the cell membranes in plants. It is also used in the seed production and pollination processes.

How to prepare the best nutrient solution for your plants

Now that you understand the basics of plant nutrients, it is time to go over how to select and prepare them. You can either purchase each of the nutrients separately and create your own proportionate blend. Or, you can purchase a ready-made fertilizer. For beginners, it is generally recommended to purchase a pre-made fertilizer and save creating your own blend for once you have more experience. A lot goes into giving plants nutrients, as you must worry about either over or underfeeding. This is only more difficult if you are a beginner and have not learned how to balance it on your own, watch for signs of trouble, or fix any problems that pop up.

When you purchase a fertilizer, it will usually tell you the percentage it has of the three main nutrients. For instance, it may look like one of these two options:

- 10-10-10
- 10% N, 10% P, 10% K

In these two examples, the phosphorus, nitrogen, and potassium each take up ten percent of the total fertilizer, for a total of thirty percent. But, what's in the additional seventy percent? This will be the other nutrients mentioned above, water, and additional chelates to help bond the molecules and improve nutrient absorption.

Of course, this is only one percentage example. The exact percentage of a given fertilizer will depend on plant type, stage of growth, season, weather, temperature, and lighting. Some fertilizers will even factor in whether you want to promote the rooting, vegetation, or fruiting of the plant.

There are many different brands you can choose from, which you can find at a local hydroponics store or online. Remember, never use fertilizers intended for soil-based gardening, even if the fertilizer doesn't contain any soil. For hydroponic gardening, you should only use hydroponic fertilizers. You can purchase these fertilizers in either dry or liquid form. If you are on a budget, you will likely use the dry form. But, if you want to prioritize ease of use, then you may choose the liquid form.

While there are many brands to choose from, and what you choose will depend on your specific needs, a few of the top selections include:

- General Hydroponics Flora Grow, Bloom, Micro Combo Fertilizer set
- General Hydroponics General Organics Go Box
- General Hydroponics Maxigro, Maxibloom
- General Hydroponics CALiMAGic Quart
- FoxFarm FX14050 Big Bloom, Grow Big & Tiger Bloom Liquid Fertilizer Nutrient Trio

Now, let's look at how you combine your fertilizer to create a nutrient solution. For this example, we will be using the three-part solution by General Hydroponics.

First, you must check what stage of growth your plants are in order to know the correct ratio. Are they in the root, vegetative, flowering, or fruiting stage? The manufacturer instructions will tell you what ratio to combine the fertilizer depending on the stage of growth. Never forget to check these instructions, no matter what brand you are using.

Add your freshwater to the reservoir. Remember to never use hard water, so you might need to first filter the water before use.

Stir the micronutrient solution portion of the fertilizer into the water until fully dissolved. This includes a small amount of nitrogen, but mainly calcium, copper, iron, zinc, manganese, and boron.

Afterward, it is time to stir in the growing portion of the fertilizer. This portion contains nitrate nitrogen, ammoniacal nitrogen, potassium, phosphate, and magnesium. Again, stir until this mixture is fully dissolved into the water.

Lastly, it is time to stir in the bloom solution. This portion contains potassium, phosphate, sulfur, and soluble magnesium. Remember, always stir each portion of the fertilizer in fully until it is dissolved.

After adding all the nutrients into the water, you must check the pH level. You can never skip this step, as if the pH level is wrong, it can stunt the growth of your plants or even kill them. The ideal range can vary, but it is generally between 5.5 and 6.5.

After everything is dissolved and the pH level is balanced, the last step is to check the temperature of your water solution. You generally want the temperature to be between 64-66°F or 18°C.

Conclusion

Hydroponics has been around literally for ages, but it is only just starting to pick up some serious interest. These gardens can take a bit of work to set up and maintain but they offer a great way of growing crops. We focused here on those looking to get started with hydroponics, so we tailored our information towards the beginner. The lessons we covered, however, have everything the beginner needs to get started and begin the road to expert.

We have six primary setups to choose from when it comes to what kind of system we want to set up. We saw how to set up deep water, wicking and drip systems. These are the easiest systems for DIY setups and beginners but there are also aeroponics, ebb and flow and nutrient film technique systems. These systems are more complicated than it is recommended for a beginner, but I encourage you to have a look at them as you get more comfortable with hydroponics.

There are four key elements that we looked at as the operation cycle of the hydroponic garden. These are soiling, seeding, lighting and trimming. By understanding how each of these elements works, we can handle the growing cycle of our plants. There are many options available for soiling and several for lighting. Finding the combination that is right for you will take some research, but it should ultimately be decided on what plants you want to grow.

Speaking of plants, we have seen that there are a ton of plants that work very well in hydroponic gardens. Herbs grown in a hydroponic garden have 30% more aromatic oils than those grown in soil. In particular lettuce absolutely adores growing hydroponically. Each plant has its own preferences when it comes to how much water it wants, the pH level it likes best and the temperature that it needs to grow. For this reason, we must research our plants and make sure that we only grow those that are compatible together.

We also learned how to mix our own nutrient solutions so that we can provide our plants with what they need to grow. There are a lot of pre-mixed options available for purchase as well. Taking control of our own mix is just another way we can get closer to our plants and provide for them to the best of our ability.

The importance of maintaining a clean garden cannot be stressed enough and so we spent time learning how we care for our gardens. The information here can be used to build your own maintenance schedule. To do this, look at how often each step of maintenance needs to be performed and plan so that you don't forget. It is super important that we take care of our plants because we don't want them in dirty environments, nor do we want them to be overly stressed. A dirty environment and a stressed plant are a recipe for infestation and infection.

We explored some of the most common pests that attack our plants. However, we didn't cover all of them. The pests we covered are the most likely ones you will have to deal with but that doesn't mean they will be the only ones. It is a good thing we also learned how to prevent pests. The preventive steps we learned will also help us to spot any pests we did not cover. If you find something you don't recognize in one of your traps then you know it is time for more research. Remember too that not every insect is a pest, some help us out by eating pests!

Infection is a risk with all gardens and so our number one tool in preventing harmful pathogens from attacking our plants is to make sure that our plants are nice and strong. We clean our gardens, we provide them with nutrients mixed to their liking, we give them the love and care they need and in doing this we keep them healthy and unstressed. While infection can still take hold in a healthy plant, it is far more likely to attack stressed plants. Finally, we looked at mistakes that are common to beginning hydroponic gardeners. We also exploded those myths that surround hydroponics to dispel the lies and untruths surrounding our newfound hobby. Searching online for tips or mistakes will reveal many discussions with hydroponic gardeners that are written specifically to help beginners like you to have the easiest, most enjoyable time possible getting into this form of gardening.

If you're excited to get started, then I suggest you begin planning out your garden now. You will need to dedicate a space for it and pick which system is most appealing to you and your skill level. Write down the plants you are most interested in growing and begin gathering information about them; what environment do they like best? What temperature? How much light do they need? What pH level?

Once you know what plants you want to grow and what system you want, you can start to build a shopping list. Along with the hardware to set up the system itself, don't forget to get some pH testing kits and an EC meter. Also make sure you have cleaning material, as you know now how important it is to sanitize and sterilize your equipment. This is also a great time to build your maintenance schedule.

The information that we covered will take you from beginner and, along with the application of practice, turn you into a pro in no time. But most importantly, don't forget to have fun!

Ingram Content Group UK Ltd.
Milton Keynes UK
UKHW051950170723
425314UK00008B/166